Interprofessional Care
and
Collaborative Practice

Interprofessional Care
and
Collaborative Practice

R. Michael Casto
María C. Juliá
Larry J. Platt
Gary L. Harbaugh
Wynne R. Waugaman
Arlene Thompson
Timothy S. Jost
Edward T. Bope
Tennyson Williams
Daniel B. Lee

COMMISSION ON INTERPROFESSIONAL EDUCATION AND PRACTICE

Brooks/Cole Publishing Company
Pacific Grove, California

I(**T**)**P** ™ The trademark ITP is used under license.

A CLAIREMONT BOOK

Brooks/Cole Publishing Company
A Division of Wadsworth, Inc.

Printed in the United States of America

10   9   8   7   6   5   4   3   2   1

Library of Congress Cataloging-in-Publication Data
Interprofessional care and collaborative practice / R. Michael Casto,
  María C. Juliá : the Commission on Interprofessional Education and
  Practice.
     p.   cm.
  Includes bibliographical references and index.
  ISBN 0-534-22236-6
  1. Social service—Team work.   2. Health care teams.   3. Helping
behavior.   I. Casto, R. Michael, [date].   II. Juliá, María C.
III. Ohio State University. Commission on Interprofessional
Education and Practice.
HV41.I555   1994
361'.068'4—dc20   93-43348
                                                                   CIP

Sponsoring Editor: *Claire Verduin*
Editorial Associate: *Gay C. Bond*
Production Editor: *Kirk Bomont*
Production Assistant: *Tessa A. McGlasson*
Manuscript Editor: *Catherine Cambron*
Interior and Cover Design: *Terri Wright*
Interior Illustration: *Susan Haberkorn*
Typesetting: *Kachina Typesetting, Inc.*
Cover Printing: *Color Dot Graphics, Inc.*
Printing and Binding: *Arcata Graphics/Fairfield*

Contents

About the Authors

EDWARD T. BOPE, M.D., is a family physician and is director of the Riverside Methodist Hospital Family Practice Residency. He is an associate clinical professor at the Ohio State University.

R. MICHAEL CASTO, M.DIV., PH.D., is director of the Interprofessional Commision of Ohio located at the Ohio State University. He writes and lectures extensively on issues related to interprofessional education and practice. He consults with academic institutions, professional associations, and public and private sector representatives about establishing interprofessional education and partnerships for collaborative practice.

GARY L. HARBAUGH, S.T.M., PH.D., completed an interdisciplinary doctorate in religion and personality (psychological studies) from the University of Chicago and a postdoctoral program in clinical psychology. He teaches pastoral care and psychology at Trinity Lutheran Seminary and founded Kairos Care and Counseling in Orlando, Florida, to support church professionals and their families.

TIMOTHY STOLTZFUS JOST, J.D., holds the Newton D. Baker and Hostetler Chair in the Ohio State University College of Law and is a professor in the Department of Hospital and Health Services Administration of the College of Medicine. He has written numerous books and articles in the area of health care law.

MARÍA C. JULIÁ, M.S.W., PH.D., is assistant professor at the Ohio State University, College of Social Work, where she also received her doctorate. Before joining the OSU faculty, she served as social work consultant for both the Ohio and Puerto Rico health departments. Dr. Juliá is actively involved in over a dozen task forces, committees, and boards where she volunteers her time. She has made numerous presentations and published several articles in the area of maternal and child health in the United States and abroad. Her research interests are in the area of maternal and child health and the role of women in international social development.

DANIEL B. LEE, D.S.W., is a professor of clinical social work and family therapy at Loyola University of Chicago School of Social Work and chairs the human behavior and social environment sequence. He taught interprofessional care courses at the Ohio State University from 1980 to 1990. His authorship includes a number of articles on life cycle issues, cross-cultural counseling, and interdisciplinary team management. He is a clinical member of the American Association for Marriage and Family Therapists and a member of the Academy of Certified Social Workers.

LARRY J. PLATT, M.D., M.P.H., is a pediatrician and preventive medicine physician. He has worked for the Health Resources and Services Administration and the National Institute of Mental Health in the U.S. Public Health Service. Most recently, he has developed national and state child health policy for the Maternal and Child Health Bureau. Currently, he is working as a private consultant on the organization and delivery of health care and program development in Berkeley, California.

ARLENE THOMPSON, R.N., PH.D., is assistant professor at the Ohio State University in the College of Nursing, Department of Community, Parent/Child and Psychiatric Nursing. She is a faculty fellow with the National Institute on Alcohol Abuse and Alcoholism. She is also a national certified counselor and a licensed professional clinical counselor. She is a noted leader, trainer, and teacher in group work and related skills. Her research and writing have focused on chemical dependency.

WYNNE R. WAUGAMAN, C.R.N.A., PH.D., is associate professor and director of the UCLA/Los Angeles County/Olive View Medical Center Program of Nurse Anesthesia in Los Angeles, California. She received her M.Ed. and Ph.D. degrees from the University of Pittsburgh and her MSN from Case Western Reserve University. Active in research and publication, she is the author of numerous articles and books. She is past president of the California Association of Nurse Anesthetists and a senior reviewer for the Council on Accreditation of Nurse Anesthesia Educational Programs. She also serves on the board of directors of the Education and Research Foundation of the American Association of Nurse Anesthetists.

P. TENNYSON WILLIAMS, M.D., is founding chair and professor emeritus of the Department of Family Medicine at the Ohio State University. He spent 22 years in private practice in family medicine in a rural college community before entering an academic career.

Introduction

Purpose and Organization

The purpose of this book is to provide materials for those engaged in learning about the dynamics, techniques, and potential of interprofessional collaboration. The book is organized according to key concepts essential to understanding and practicing interprofessional collaboration. Eight case studies thread their way through most chapters to unify and illustrate the text.

Part One, "A Way of Perceiving," addresses the theoretical framework that forms the basis for interprofessional collaboration. This part of the book reviews basic assumptions, the context for collaborative practice, relevant research and literature, and the ways professionals enter their vocations.

Part Two, "A Way of Understanding," presents both an overview and an in-depth discussion of group process. The history, basic assumptions, and essential elements of interprofessional teamwork are explored and integrated.

Part Three, "A Way of Responding," discusses methodologies for interprofessional practice. This section considers models for collaboration, the processes of interprofessional teamwork, and educational goals and methodologies. Part Three ends with a description and discussion of interprofessional policy analysis.

Part Four, "Resources," provides case studies and selected codes of professional ethics. Related interprofessional activities for students, teachers, and professionals are also suggested. These activities are designed to assist prospective teachers, clergy, social workers, physicians, lawyers, and other human service professionals in becoming more effective interprofessional practitioners.

Part Five, "Reflections," presents a model program for interprofessional education and practice. A detailed review of the process of writing this book serves as a case study in interprofessional collaboration.

A Word About How This Book Came to Be

In 1985, a group of faculty members met to define and outline a project to interprofessionally develop resources that could be used in learning the skills, processes, and structures necessary to support interprofessional collaboration. This book reflects both the effort of these faculty members and the collaborative process they engaged in for more than six years. A unique feature of this collaborative endeavor and its product is that each chapter not only discusses but also reflects an interprofessional process and perspective. Although written by individual authors, each contribution was reviewed by all the other members of the writing team. The authors then incorporated into their individual chapters the feedback they received from the variety of professional perspectives represented by the other participating faculty members. This procedure was repeated several times during the writing process, resulting in a uniquely interprofessional and collaborative product, rather than a mere collection of essays. The writing team also unified the book by illustrating the text with the cases found in Chapter 10.

The text, therefore, exhibits a variety of perspectives and styles rather than a single unified perspective. This variety reflects the realities of professional practice in a collaborative, interprofessional context. It also reflects the realities of the truly interprofessional classroom. The authors believe that this variety adds strength and truth to both the content of the text and the collaborative context in which it was written.

Throughout the project, the group provided its own leadership. It operated as a consensus group and took full advantage of the opportunity to practice and experience interprofessional collaboration during the writing process. The Commission on Interprofessional Education and Practice provided staff support for the project. The staff facilitated the work of the group by caring for its organizational life, providing materials as requested, and offering some research assistance. One staff member also participated in the group as a contributor on the same basis as other faculty members. The collaborative writing effort would have been much more difficult if it had not been facilitated by an administrative structure and the work of effective staff.

Contributors

All the faculty members listed in this section have contributed in a major way to the shape of this project with written materials and through their active participation in the process. The faculty come from several sessions of the

Seminar on Interprofessional Care, which has been offered over many years by the participating academic units. At the beginning of the project, there was some mobility among those faculty members who participated; some became regular group members, while others decided to focus their energies elsewhere.[1] The team represents a number of different practice and teaching disciplines as well as a wide variety of professional training and experience. The team also represents a wide variety of socioeconomic, cultural, ethnic, and geographic characteristics. We believe this diversity is also a strength in our increasingly heterogeneous society.

> *Interprofessional education:* R. Michael Casto, M.Div., Ph.D.
> *Law:* Timothy S. Jost, J.D.
> *Family medicine:* Edward T. Bope, M.D.; P. Tennyson Williams, M.D.
> *Nurse anesthesiology:* Wynne R. Waugaman, C.R.N.A., Ph.D.
> *Nursing:* Arlene Thompson, R.N., Ph.D.
> *Pastoral care and psychology:* Gary L. Harbaugh, S.T.M., Ph.D.
> *Pediatrics and public health:* Larry J. Platt, M.D., M.P.H
> *Social work:* María C. Juliá, M.S.W., Ph.D.; Daniel B. Lee, D.S.W.

One regret of the writing team was the absence of a teacher educator in our midst. In an effort to remedy this lamentable deficiency, the team invited Frederick R. Cyphert, professor and dean emeritus of the College of Education at the Ohio State University, to serve as reviewer, critic, and consultant to the project. As an experienced faculty member in the Seminar on Interprofessional Care, Dr. Cyphert made invaluable contributions through his observations, comments, and helpful critiques.

One common characteristic of those who participated in shaping and writing this text is that all have taught in the Seminar on Interprofessional Care at one time or another. All members of the group share a concern that materials be made available to teach the skills necessary for effective interprofessional collaboration. They all have experienced the difficulty of teaching without effective teaching materials. And perhaps most significantly, the members of the group have each accumulated through their teaching experience a wealth of knowledge about the subjects they teach. The faculty members are each respected teachers in their own fields. Each has also experienced the importance of interprofessional collaboration for effective professional practice.

Many of the faculty members have had long experience as practitioners, and some continue their practice as they teach. They bring to the classroom and the text the important perspective of those who have both practiced in their field and taught in their respective professional schools. For them, the theoretical material presented in this book reflects the realities of professional practice and the need for an interprofessional approach to many of the complex problems of

---

[1] Eleanor P. Nystrom, occupational therapy; Roberta Sands, social work; and Thoralf Thielen, theology.

people in our society. As practitioners, many of the faculty have been involved in collaborative professional practice as well as collaborative education. They believe that interprofessional practice enhances the quality of service delivered to clients and enriches practitioners' own professional life.

This book is the product of the collaboration of many individuals. It would not have been produced without the ongoing support of the board of directors and staff of the Commission on Interprofessional Education and Practice at the Ohio State University. A number of persons reviewed the manuscript at various stages in its development. Our deep appreciation goes to Frederick R. Cyphert and Anne S. Allen, both retired from the Ohio State University; James L. Williamson, Baylor University; and John R. Snyder, Indiana University–Purdue University at Indianapolis. Each made significant contributions in their critique and review of our work. The faculty who wrote and reviewed each chapter remain indebted to their colleagues and families for their insights and patience. Finally, on a personal note, we would like to thank Sally, Andrew, Daniel, and Jim for their continued love, support, and encouragement throughout our work.

R. Michael Casto
María C. Juliá

PART 1

A Way of Perceiving

A Framework for
Interprofessional Care
and
Collaborative Practice

CHAPTER 1

Why Bother with Teams?
An Overview

Larry J. Platt, M.D., M.P.H.

When Dr. Mary Smith, a young physician, was employed recently to work at a neighborhood health center, she joined "Team F," which included a team nurse, a team outreach worker, and a team secretary. She was told she was part of a team of multiple disciplines and that its members should work like a team. She tried; they all tried. They had team meetings once a week, and everyone came and complained to one another about administrative issues. They more or less gossiped about some of the more difficult or noncompliant patients. They had team potluck dinners. They had team name tags. They had a team structure. But they did not function like a team—they did not know how.

TEAMS AND CULTURAL INDIVIDUALISM

The difficulty Team F had in functioning like a team is not surprising. Everything in U.S. culture conduces to individualism. Even our sports teams are portrayed as collections of individuals whose star quality and contract provisions vary. We know more about individual statistics than about the intricacies of team interaction and function. We are socialized in our culture to simple answers, isolated variables, and competitive values. These values and frameworks underlie our art, our media, our advertising, our teaching, our professional training—everything about U.S. society. No wonder Dr. Smith and her colleagues did not know how to work like a team; they did not even know how to think like a team.

A team is a team by virtue not so much of numbers but of process—the interactions among individuals gathered toward some end.

The fact that interactions among individuals are involved means of course that a team has to involve at least two members. John Wayne riding into the sunset, Clint Eastwood rubbing out a revolution, Rambo rescuing the world, are obviously not examples of teams. But even if the characters portrayed by Wayne, Eastwood, and Stallone were to work in some future production on saving Metropolis together, they would not necessarily be a team—not unless they interacted in a way that made the group more functional in terms of its mission than the sum of the individual talents would suggest.

REQUIREMENTS AND PROCESSES

Thus, a team requires (a) a group of two or more people, (b) a shared sense of purpose or purposes among the group members, and (c) interactions among the members that make them able to accomplish more than each would be able to accomplish working individually toward the shared purpose. Each of these factors is necessary to enable a functioning interdisciplinary team; none is sufficient without the others.

The interactions involved when a team works like a team include processes internal to the team and other processes that relate to how the group interacts with the world outside the team. The internal processes include *communicating*—exchanging information; *problem-solving*—defining issues and devising a response to them; *decision-making*—resolving how differences are accommodated and power is distributed; *conflict resolution*—working out disputes; and *maintenance*—engaging in activities that develop and maintain among members (including new members) group identity, responsibility, mutual support, and integrity.

Interacting with the outside world involves an interdisciplinary team in such processes as *coordination* of plans, partnerships, and resources; *referring and consulting* with other individuals and groups about problems of mutual interest; *fulfilling institutional functions* in the larger group or community; *adapting, developing* functionally, *surviving,* and *dying* as a group organism; *coming to an understanding,* if not an agreement, on contextual rules, laws, norms, and roles and on ways to negotiate or establish changes in those rules, laws, norms, and roles; and *sharing information* required for working effectively with others. Sometimes it is the team's interactions with the outer world that

make the team's purpose clearer, define who is on the team, and help the interactions of the group conduce to a team.

Engaging in these processes, both internal and external, takes lots of work. It also takes time and some commitment on the part of a critical number of team members—at least two or three.

WHY TEAMS?

So why bother with teams?

The first of two basic reasons one might have to join or develop a team is that the rules for achieving a given purpose require it. Baseball calls for nine players on a team. Playing bridge requires a partner; playing it successfully requires a partnership. And some institutions mandate group approaches to certain problems or functional areas, such as ethics.

The second reason is that an issue, problem, function, or situation may be such that a team will work better than an individual or a bunch of individuals. The need for a team approach to the delivery of human services has become more and more evident as the problems confronting those in the helping professions become more complex. Most of the simpler problems have been selected out by solution, and our understanding of the nature of problems, specifically and generally, has become more intricate. The need for a team approach has become more evident as providers have become increasingly specialized in order to bring technological depth to practice. And the need for a team approach has become more evident as the system of programs and agencies created to address human problems has become increasingly categorical and fragmented.

In health, the nature of problems related to the so-called new morbidity— chronic disease, emotional problems, recurrent illness—and an appreciation of the interaction among social, emotional, and biologic factors require both a new framework for problem analysis and a new way of practice. *Systems theory* provides the framework for analysis (see Chapter 7), and a *team approach* provides a method for practice.

Historically, the concept of health is grounded in a taxonomy of diseases. The definition of health as the absence of disease pervades our medical system, our reimbursement system, our delivery system, our surveillance system, and even much of our public health system.

Similar understandings pervade other disciplines. Any given individual may not be at risk from the point of view of a professional if that individual does not manifest the deficits that concern that particular profession.

An alternative view of health would define it as a state with the following characteristics:

■ the ability to perform personally valued family, work, and community roles

■ the ability to deal with physical, biological, and social stress
■ a feeling of well-being
■ development through life in accordance with one's potential
■ freedom from any unusually high risk of disease and untimely death

From this understanding, a few things follow. First, the consequent scope of health services is broad, encompassing much more than just medical or clinical services. Second, health services have to be thought of in terms of development. Finally, the concept of health needs to include an appreciation of the community and culture in which a person and a family live.

One more insight devolves from this view of health. The disabilities affecting people now are different in nature and complexity from the disabilities people were thinking about when health was viewed primarily in terms of disease. In the coming years, people working in human services have to grapple with the fact that the major disabilities have nothing to do with disease.

TEAMS AND THE COMPLEXITY OF MODERN PROBLEMS

The case examples in Chapter 10 may seem atypical, but in fact, most problems confronting human service workers are complex.

Homicide, not even in the top 10 in the middle of this century, is now the fourth leading cause of death for children in the United States. It is the second leading cause of death for young adolescents, except for black male teenagers, for whom it is the leading cause of death. Both black and white male youth die from homicide more often than from all natural causes of death—the diseases we spend so much time and money on—combined. During every 100 hours on the streets in the United States we lose three times as many young men as were killed in the 100 hours of ground war in the Persian Gulf.

Adolescent white males have replaced the elderly as the group with the highest suicide rate. Suicide is now the second leading cause of death for older adolescents, just nosing out homicide.

Of youths ages 18 to 21; 17 percent—more than one in six of our children—have not completed high school. What could be more disabling?

Cocaine in the form of crack is epidemic among children; and in Detroit, 27 percent of those arrested for pushing it are under the age of 17. Alcohol is now the leading beverage among college students, who guzzle 34 gallons of alcohol per person per year.

Each year, 10 percent of all teenage girls in the United States get pregnant. That's 3,000 girls getting pregnant every day. Every hour of every day a 13- or 14-year-old has her first baby; every 2 hours, a 16-year-old has her second.

In a recent Rhode Island survey of 1700 sixth to ninth graders, 87 percent of the boys and 79 percent of the girls said that rape is OK if a couple is married; two thirds of the boys and half the girls said forced sex was acceptable if a couple had been dating for 6 months.

Medical, dental, and nutritional diseases are important. But you can't immunize against accidents and homicides; you can't mouth-rinse them away. Being a health practitioner in the present-day world means concerning oneself with the development of children and the family, as well as with immunizations; with the ability of individuals and families to adapt to the stresses of the environment, as well as with physical exams; with freedom from hunger as well as with vitamin deficiencies. To carry out that responsibility effectively, providers need to be intimately familiar with, if not integrated into, the community and environment of the child and family with whose health they are dealing.

Supporting and carrying out community-based interventions—such as education, community organization, environmental health, advocacy, agricultural co-ops, and so on—may be as much a part of the health component a program attempts to fashion, through partnerships, as is finding a niche within the structure of medical specialties.

Even when a program does focus just on diseases, the problem is no longer simple (if it ever was). The incidence of measles, congenital rubella, congenital syphilis, and AIDS is going up. Each of these is a preventable health problem. But each disease is not only a medical problem, but also a political and cultural one.

In the United States, it is estimated that half of the infants who die before reaching their first birthday need not have died. This health problem is not simply a medical or a nutritional problem, but also an economic one.

The leading cause of death after the first year is unintentional injuries. Most injuries in young children occur at home. For older children, most injuries occur at school. And many of these are preventable. But how many times has anyone gone into homes or into schools to diagnose the environment and prescribe ways to prevent these accidents?

A physician or nurse or any other individual provider simply cannot take care of these sorts of problems alone; he or she needs to be working in partnership with other workers in and from the community, as well as with the client and his or her family. And any one program cannot do it alone; it needs to work in partnership with other agencies and programs with common agendas.

TEAMS IN SYSTEMS OF SERVICE

From the point of view of the individual client, the service "system" includes multiple kinds of access points and providers and services that invariably cross agency and funding source lines. As one works with families to assist them in learning to solve problems and use resources and services in the community, one inevitably encounters difficulties related to inadequate interactions among agencies: complicated eligibility requirements, repetitive intake, conflicting service plans, poor follow-up on referrals, ignorance of relevant community and family resources, agency disagreements about funding responsibilities, and poor ability to assess community problems and priorities for allocation of resources. Paradoxically, the more services a family needs, the less effective the system becomes. The number of agencies in a community is almost always great enough to make the system require deliberate and explicit management, which is what is usually missing.

Given the need to address the system coupled with the difficulty in doing so, it is no wonder that multiple attempts have been made to address systemic issues in the delivery of health and human services, fostering a rich vocabulary. Attempts have been made to coordinate, integrate, network, build teams, plan comprehensively, develop systems, case manage, and consider one-stop super-markets of care.

It is also little wonder that so many of these attempts have been short-lived successes or outright failures. Health insurance programs rarely support the most effective health services and are not designed to support the kind of solutions required by most health problems these days—problems such as chronic illness, substance abuse, violence, emotional illness, accident preven-tion, illiteracy, and learning disorders. Solutions for these problems involve multiple and complex human-to-human interactions. We know little about such interactions, and if any significant research effort concerning them is being made, it is minimal.

A functional system of care would be conversant with the language and culture of different agencies; it would have mechanisms for integrating work involving multiple providers; it would have a means for making decisions involving multiple decision-makers and working out funding of care involving multiple sources; it would have a mechanism for defining standards against which to program and evaluate comprehensive interventions; and it would have a means for holding the community and its families in primary focus even as the administrative rigmarole demands near-total attention.

TEAM MANAGEMENT AND SPECIALIZATION

Even as problems become more complicated and our understanding of them more profound and complex, those trying to effect solutions are becoming more specialized. So more and more people need to be involved in the solution of any problem. But professionals are not trained to work together. Our cultural values do not support that ideal, and the service structures to facilitate in-teractions are sparse to nonexistent.

With increased specialization, the person as client is divided up by body part, by physiologic system, by disease, and by intervention to be applied. And there are professions within professions to deal with each division. Some mechanism for getting the person back together conceptually is necessary, not only for humanistic reasons, but also because problems are not usually so divisible. One solution has been to redefine the role of the generalist or primary care provider to include the function of integration or case management. Ironically, one answer to the problem of specialization has been the development of another specialist, the so-called case manager.

With or without a primary care provider serving as manager or a special case manager serving as a coordinator, the need to integrate the views, prescriptions, and plans of the specialists within and across professions requires interactions among those varied providers. In other words, what is called for is a *team*. What is also required is a functional, multiagency system. Both these things are so inconsistent with the traditions of American culture that they will not evolve without the specific planning of services and training of providers.

The questions who should be on the team, how the team may carry out the purpose of integration and coordination of elements related to a given client, what structure the team may use to engage the interactive processes outlined in this section, and how the team may achieve the potential synergistic benefits derived from those interactions are the subject of the rest of this book.

REFERENCES AND RELATED READINGS

Baldwin, D. C., Jr. (1982). The British are coming: some observations on health care teams in Great Britain. In Pisaneschi, J. (Ed.), *Interdisciplinary health team care: Proceedings of the Fourth Annual Conference*. Lexington, KY: Center for Interdisciplinary Education, University of Kentucky.

Baldwin, D. C., Jr., and Tsukuda, R. A. W. (1984). Interdisciplinary teams. In Cassel, C., and Walsh, J. R. (Eds.), *Geriatric medicine, volume II: Fundamentals of geriatric care*. New York: Springer-Verlag, 1984.

Casto, R. M. (1992). The turmoil of turf: Interprofessional collaboration in the war zone. In Snyder, J. R. (Ed.), *Interdisciplinary health care teams: Proceedings of the Thirteenth Annual Conference* (pp. 198–204). Indianapolis: School of Allied Health Sciences, Indiana University School of Medicine, Indiana University Medical Center.

Kolb, J. A. (1992). Leadership of creative teams. *Journal of Creative Behavior, 26* (1), 1–9.

Masters, L. F. (1992). *Supervision for successful team leadership: A personal analysis—The questions and answers you need to know*. Las Vegas: Achievement Press International.

Melaville, A. I., and Blank, M. J. (1991). *What it takes: Structuring interagency partnerships to connect children and families with comprehensive services*. Washington, DC: Education and Human Services Consortium.

Opper, S. (1992). *Technology for teams: Enhancing productivity in network organizations*. New York: Van Nostrand Reinhold.

Rees, F. (1991). *How to lead work teams: Facilitation skills*. San Diego: Pfeiffer and Co.

Shonk, J. H. (1992). *Team based organizations: Developing a successful team environment.* Homewood, IL: Business One Irwin.

Wilber, M. M. (1992). *Three is a team: Collaborative consultation techniques for educators.* Paper presented at the Midwest Symposium for Leadership in Behavior Disorders, Kansas City, MO.

CHAPTER 2

Assumptions of Interprofessional Collaboration
Interrelatedness and Wholeness

Gary L. Harbaugh, S.T.M., Ph.D.

CASES AND ASSUMPTIONS

Almost 70 years old, Olga wandered around town during a light snowfall. When found by the police, she could tell them her name but not her address.

Roger and Jay had been lovers, then broke up. After Jay met and married Peggy, he no longer would speak to Roger. When later Roger became ill, and his type of pneumonia strongly suggested AIDS, Roger did not want to tell Jay what was suspected.

Jimmie has become increasingly withdrawn since he told his father what his uncle made him do. Jimmie's father refused to listen to what Jimmie said had happened.

Jessica is married to a church deacon who drinks heavily. He doesn't remember pushing his wife down the stairs.

If you were a helping professional, and Olga or Roger or any of the others came to you for assistance, you would ask for more information. To make a helpful response, you would need to know all relevant details and interpret their relevance accurately (see Chapter 10 for case studies).

The message of this book is that, regardless of how much information any one helping professional would be able to gather, interprofessional collaboration in cases like these has the best chance of resulting in appropriate and effective human services and caregiving.

To help you understand why we believe interprofessional collaboration is so desirable and powerful, this chapter will discuss the nature of the helping-caring relationship, the characteristics of many of those who are interprofessionally-oriented helping professionals, and the assumptions that people drawn to helping professions usually have in common. Finally, we'll look at some implications our observations have for professional practice. The chapters that follow will detail these implications more fully and suggest practical guidelines for the kind of interprofessional collaboration that we think would lead to a more effective response to people like Olga, Roger, Jimmie, and Jessica.

THE HELPING-CARING RELATIONSHIP

We define a helping professional as a professionally trained person who provides professional and personal services to individuals, groups, and social systems with the intent of improving their quality of life. Characteristically, helping professionals are interested in the prevention of human problems. When prevention is not possible and problems already exist, helping professionals provide assessment, encouragement, support, alternatives, and—where needed and possible—healing.

The services of a helping professional are professional and personal. They are *professional* inasmuch as they are based on a body of expert knowledge, the integration of which ordinarily requires the professional to undergo an extensive period of academic preparation (Carlton, 1984). Human services are also *personal,* since they are typically people-oriented—whether offered in individual situations, group or community settings, or at the systemic or societal (macro) level.

Despite some commonalities in definition, not all helping professionals share the same assumptions about how best to help people in need of services. Not only do different professions take different approaches, but within any given profession there are differences of opinion about the relative merits of alternative treatment strategies. Nevertheless, many helping professionals share certain broad assumptions about people. When professionals recognize the significant areas of agreement between them and helping professionals in other disciplines, then it is more likely that they will recognize the value of interprofessional collaboration.

What assumptions seem to cross the boundaries of the helping professions? One assumption many helping professionals share is that the world is characterized by interpersonal interrelatedness. An increasing number of professionals in a wide variety of helping professions have used the word *holistic* to denote this interrelatedness.

This assumption leads us to ask two questions. First, how does the kind of interrelatedness that helping professionals perceive differ from how the world looks to those in other vocations? Second, how does professional practice change when the world is seen in this way?

THE HELPING PERSON'S WORLDVIEW

One way to view the world is as the environment in which we live. As an environment, the world is a physical world of space and time, subject to the laws and balances of nature. It is a material world of objects and things. It is an objective world of cause and effect that individuals need to understand in order to gain as much control as possible.

Helping professionals live in the physical, material, and objective world just as everyone else does. But for most helping professionals, the world is not primarily defined in such objective terms. For the world to be truly understood, helping professionals believe the world must also be perceived as a world of others. The world is more than an environment. Objectivity must be balanced with subjectivity, the material with the relational, the physical with the psychosocial.

Because helping professionals view the world in this way, for them interpersonal relationships are relatively more significant than for those in many other vocations, such as engineering or accounting. Accordingly, helping professionals are more likely to perceive a problem situation as one in which *people* are having problems. Problem-solving, therefore, must not only solve the objective problem, but also make good "people sense."

Helping professionals perceive that complex human problems need a personal approach and emphasize the importance of the relationship between the caregiver and the person or people receiving care as an integral part of the problem-solving process. In medicine, for example, the so-called placebo effect illustrates how powerfully the patient's relationship with the helping professional contributes to the healing process.

PERSONALITY AND PERCEPTION

Why are helping professionals more likely than other types of professionals to be keenly conscious of the relational character of life? One interpretation of their greater degree of people orientation is that the personality preferences of those in helping professions are typically different from the personality preferences of those in other vocations. To put it another way, what is seen is related to who is doing the seeing, or the personality of the perceiver.

The research coming out of studies that use the Myers-Briggs Type Indicator (MBTI) supports this interpretation. The MBTI is based on Jungian psychology, which identifies differing orientations to the world (extraversion versus introversion). The MBTI indicates not only extraversion and introversion, but also an individual's preferred way of living; for example, some have a personality preference for a more orderly and organized life-style, in contrast to those whose predisposition is toward an adaptive style of "going with the flow."

As important as life-style and orientation to the outer and inner worlds is, Jung placed greatest emphasis on an individual's preferred way of seeing and deciding (Jung's words were *perception* and *judgment*). Jung believed that some people see primarily with their senses and others with a sixth sense, or intuition. After seeing, a decision must be made about what one sees. Jung said some people decide with thinking judgment, making decisions based on objective, logical analysis of a problem. Others decide with feeling judgment, which is equally rational; for these people, however, the bottom line is person-centered values rather than logic (Myers with Myers, 1980; Myers and McCaulley, 1985).

Helping professionals may have any of these personality characteristics, since no one personality type always makes a superior helping professional (just as no personality type is always inappropriate in the helping professions). In addition, just because a person has a personality preference does not mean that person is good at what she or he prefers. For example, for someone to prefer extraversion does not necessarily mean that the person is an effective extravert, and someone who does not have a personality preference for extraversion may, when necessary, be quite an effective extravert. Because success cannot be predicted on the basis of MBTI results, denying admission to a helping profession based on the MBTI or a similar preference indicator is unethical. Used as a screening instrument, the MBTI would unfairly exclude some outstanding candidates.

On the other hand, interprofessional research suggests that most of those who are attracted to helping professions seem to have some personality preferences in common. One of these is a higher than expected preference for a more feeling, person-centered approach to problems (Harbaugh, 1984a, 1984b, 1985; Myers and McCaulley, 1985).

Interesting results are reported by Myers and McCaulley based on a series of studies that sampled 9,204 helping professionals in the United States. To interpret the research, it must be noted that approximately 40 percent of the general male population and 60 percent of the general female population has a preference for making what the MBTI calls "feeling" (or person-centered) decisions (Myers with Myers, 1980), and the percentage of male as compared with the percentage of female practitioners varies from profession to profession. With these guidelines to be used for their interpretation, the studies show that physicians as a total group average a feeling preference of 51 percent; psychiatrists 54 percent; psychologists 55 percent; health care therapists 59 percent; family practice physicians 63 percent; registered nurses, medical assistants, and social workers all around 64 percent; counselors 66 percent; general health service workers 67 percent; public health nurses 70 percent; and clergy (all denominations) 79 percent (Myers and McCaulley, 1985).

These research results do not suggest that helping professionals should have a preference for feeling judgment, but rather that the majority of those who work in the helping professions display strong leanings toward making decisions on the basis of person-centered values. In every helping profession cited, with male-female differences taken into consideration, the percentage of feeling types of people exceeded what would be expected based on this percentage in the general population.

How does the greater feeling preference of most helping professionals show up in clinical practice? One expression of feeling preference is the therapeutic or facilitating value placed on the interpersonal relationship between the helping professional and the person seeking help. A related indication of the influence of a feeling preference is the significance most helping professionals would attach to the nature and the quality of Olga's or Roger's or Jimmie's or Jessica's interpersonal relationships (in the present and also in the past).

Looking at the world in terms of interrelatedness and interrelationships may reflect the predominant feeling preference of many helping professionals, but this worldview may also reflect more than that. Since not all helping professionals are feeling types, their tendency to look at a problem from the perspective of interrelatedness and interrelationships may arise from something else. Let's look at a second assumption commonly shared by those helping professionals drawn to interprofessional collaboration—that is, the assumption that persons are most appropriately understood holistically.

Holistic Assumptions of Helping Professionals

The word *holistic* (sometimes spelled *wholistic*) can mean different things to different people, but usually it represents an attempt to look as comprehensively as possible at what it is to be human. Because it is sometimes easier to picture wholeness than to describe it, frequently a model is developed. Contemporary models of wholeness, such as that shown in Figure 2.1, are often individual models that highlight the interaction of a person's body, mind, feelings, and relationships (Harbaugh, 1984a).

The model in Figure 2.1 may be similar to others in that, while the labels vary, most individual holistic models identify the physical, mental, emotional, and social dimensions of life. The model in Figure 2.1 is unique in that it arranges these familiar dimensions in such a way as to meet in the center at the point of a common *L* (Harbaugh, 1976, 1983, 1984a). The purpose of this arrangement is to serve as a reminder that what happens in any one area

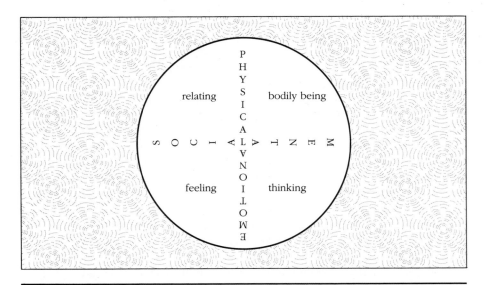

FIGURE 2.1 ■
A model of wholeness   (© Gary L. Harbaugh, 1976, 1983, 1984)

of life will affect every other dimension of a person's humanness. For example, how a person thinks (mentally) and feels (physically and emotionally) is interrelated with the way that person relates and acts. The physical, mental, emotional, and social dimensions of life are all involved when we think about a person. Olga's wandering around in a snowfall unable to tell the police her address not only raised a question about her mental well-being but also had implications for her physical well-being. Roger's decision not to tell Jay about his medical condition potentially affected not only Jay's health but also had implications that could seriously affect Jay's interpersonal relationship with his wife. Keep the holistic model in mind as you review the cases of Olga, Roger, Jimmie, and Jessica in Chapter 10.

On the holistic model, the central *L* not only represents the interrelationship and interaction of the four dimensions, but also serves a deeper purpose. The central *L* stands for the integration of all these dimensions in our personal values. Since *L* is the central letter of the word *value,* placing an *L* at the center of this model is a way of saying that values are always involved in anything that affects a person's body, mind, feelings, or relationships. Values, reflected in priorities, underlie the ways in which we care for our physical needs, develop our intellects, strengthen our capacities to feel for and feel with others, and respond to others. Roger's values were involved in his decision not to inform Jay, as Jay's were involved in his earlier decision not to tell his wife-to-be about his past relationship with Roger.

As you review the details of the case studies in Chapter 10, you will be aware that the values involved in these cases are not only those of the clients (patients, parishioners) involved, but also those of the helping professionals. Values are always involved in the choices that people make, and those values

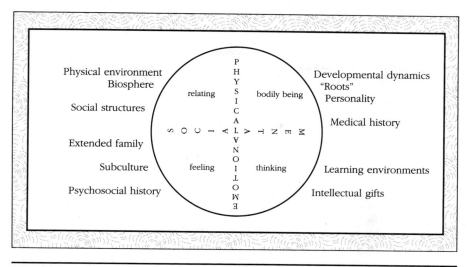

FIGURE 2.2 ■
Model of an individual in context   (© Gary L. Harbaugh)

usually are all the more apparent if viable alternatives are available to a person or professional.

Recognizing that people are *whole* people—embodied, thinking, feeling, relating, and valuing people—the interprofessionally oriented helping professional is less likely to be satisfied with approaches that are aimed at fixing a part of a human problem. Even though they may not feel competent to address all the problems themselves, holistically oriented helping persons are aware that when any part of a person's life is in trouble, the whole person (as well as the relational system in which the person lives) experiences the pain.

Any model has its limitations. For example, the model we have described has a clear application to individual, person-centered caregiving, but is it as adequate for working with groups of individuals or with larger social systems? To depict not only the intrapsychic and interpersonal but also the societal implications of the model requires additional elaboration, which is set out in Figure 2.2.

The more expanded version of the model depicts the individual within the context of many systems and forces that affect his or her situation ecologically. From the family of origin (developmental roots, psychosocial history, subculture, and extended family), through the socialization process in the school system (learning environments) and the overall societal structure, individuals like Olga or Roger can be perceived in relation to increasingly larger circles and spheres of influence. From the human point of view even the biosphere and inanimate environment is inevitably viewed from a subjective and personal point of view, with attention to how that environment might impact the human community. Therefore, in whatever direction we expand the model, the central theme is constant: whatever events happen in any one dimension or area of life inevitably interrelate and interact with events and conditions in all the other dimensions.

There are other ways to represent the totality of factors and forces—whether physical, psychological, psychosocial, economic, political, sociocultural, or spiritual—that ecologically impact the human situation. For example, in the medical profession, the principle of interrelatedness and interaction is seen in relation to disease (Medalie, Kitson, and Zyzanski, 1981). Disease involves the interaction of the host and the environment (the environment includes the microenvironment—that is, individual biological factors; and the macroenvironment—that is, geophysical and sociocultural factors). Out of the continuous interaction of host and environment over time comes disease or health.

Expanding in the direction of families, Medalie et al. (1981) focus on the interaction of the family system, the environment (geophysical, psychosocial, cultural, and economic), and situational stressors (life events like marriage, a death in the family, or disease). Such expansions from individual illness to family dysfunction suggest that other macro social issues may beneficially be approached from an interactive, multisystemic, and multidimensional perspective.

Whatever model or method is chosen, the point is that helping professionals are drawn to a worldview that perceives the interrelatedness of life and the constant interaction between the individual and the environment. Such perceptions inevitably affect the way that professionals practice.

IMPLICATIONS FOR PROFESSIONAL PRACTICE

A relational way of looking at the world and a holistic worldview have important implications for helping professionals. Even in the absence of interprofessional collaboration, a helping professional who is relationally and holistically oriented will try to be sensitive to people's multidimensionality. For example, a social worker with an appreciation for wholeness will respond not just to the individual in isolation, but to the individual in the context of that person's relationships. The holistically oriented nurse is aware not only of the physical needs of the patient, but also of the importance of a supportive family. The minister attending to the whole person is aware that physical illness as well as a parishioner's values may affect how that parishioner looks at life and how he or she handles interpersonal relationships.

While it is helpful for a single helping professional to try to respond to the person as a whole person, the limits of time and training and personality preferences make it difficult to do as thorough and competent a job as would be possible if the work were carried out in consultation with other professionals. Further, if consultation could enrich the professional practice of individual caregivers, might the care be even more effective if active interprofessional collaboration were taking place?

The goal of a helping profession is to move from providing merely appropriate care to providing optimal care. Helping professionals are trained to provide appropriate care. If someone has stomach spasms, going to a physician is an appropriate choice; after diagnostic tests to rule out underlying pathology are completed, for the physician to prescribe antispasmodic medicine would also seem appropriate. But if the stomach spasms are symptomatic of a disrupted interpersonal relationship, then the relief of the physical problem, however appropriate, is not fully adequate to the need of that individual as a whole person.

Similarly, if a demographic area has a much higher than expected incidence of divorce, school dropouts, and alcoholism and other drug abuse, it may be appropriate for a community mental health center to sponsor preventive educational programs that help people prevent or at least identify as early as possible the signs and symptoms that suggest the need for counseling. However appropriate such programs might be, however, such a response would not be an optimal one if the marital discord and other problems resulted from a major economic upheaval and attendant social changes affecting that locality. In that event, the mental health center along with other helping professionals might also need to enter into consultation and planning with governmental officials and industry representatives.

At both the micro and the macro level, appropriate care can be lifted to the level of optimal care by means of a conscious decision to let holistic assumptions guide professional practice. Based on such a holistic worldview, only a multifaceted approach to human problems is truly adequate. Interprofessional cooperation and care is a conscious step toward the provision of services that are both appropriate and adequate to the needs of those being served.

Interprofessional Collaboration

A rose by any other name may smell as sweet, but not all terms used to describe professional collaboration are interchangeable (Carlton, 1984). Three crucial terms are *multiprofessional, transprofessional,* and *interprofessional.* The term *multiprofessional* implies only that more than one profession is interested in a particular problem. Multiprofessional approaches are "consultative and sequential, but noninteractive" (Allen, Casto, and Janata, 1985).

The term *transprofessional* goes further, suggesting that professionals are engaged in work that embraces a number of professions. But like *multiprofessional, transprofessional* really says nothing about the nature of any collaboration (Carlton, 1984).

The term that Thomas Carlton suggests as the most accurate way of describing what most helping professionals have in mind when they talk about working together with other professionals is *interprofessional.* Helping professionals who work together, with intention, mutual respect, and commitment, for the sake of a more adequate response to a human problem are working interprofessionally.

Rosalie Kane summarizes several other current definitions of interprofessional teamwork, noting the common identifying elements in each: "All definitions allude to common purpose, separate skills or professional contributions, and some process of communication, coordination, cooperation, or joint thinking. . . . The three elements of a common objective, differential professional contributions, and a system of communication [are] considered necessary for an interprofessional team to exist" (Kane, 1983; Ducanis and Golin, 1979). An interprofessional approach does not blur the distinctiveness of each profession, but it does break through the extreme role specialization that fails to appreciate the kind of balance and integration that a holistic orientation requires (Falck, 1977).

As pointed out earlier, interprofessional approaches include, but frequently go beyond, helping people in individual or interpersonal situations of need. An interprofessional perspective on problems often leads to an identification of macro issues that require collaborative strategies for prevention, early detection, or intervention at the systemic or societal level. The cases of Olga and Roger are examples of situations where interprofessional collaboration requires attention to policy development, or at least a concern to moderate the various pressures that adversely affect individuals' lives.

Summary

Because the worldview of the helping professional is most likely to be based on a perception of the interrelatedness of life, and the assumptions that underlie that worldview are holistic assumptions, the helping professional needs to acquire skill in looking at situations from a variety of points of view. However, all perspectives are partial, and personality preferences may make it even more difficult to see a situation from certain angles. Interprofessional collaboration is a particularly effective way of approaching a situation of need from multiple points of view.

The word *interprofessional* implies interaction. Interprofessional care takes seriously the multidimensional and multisystemic nature of human problems and offers an appropriate response, all the while realizing that a truly adequate response will require the services of interprofessional colleagues. As Carlton (1984), Kane (1983), Ducanis and Golin (1979), and others point out, a commitment to interaction and good communication are the keys to successful interprofessional teamwork. Working together at micro and macro levels, interprofessionally oriented helping professionals assess, encourage, support, provide alternatives, and, where possible, lead those who are in need to higher levels of personal and systemic integration and wholeness.

REFERENCES AND RELATED READINGS

Allen, A. S., Casto, R. M., and Janata, M. M. (1985). Interprofessional practice. In Allen, A. S. (Ed.), *New options, new dilemmas* (pp. 103–111). Lexington, VA: Lexington Books.

Carlton, T. O. (1984). *Clinical social work in health settings.* New York: Springer Publishing.

Ducanis, A. J., and Golin, A. K. (1979). *The interdisciplinary health care team.* London: Aspen Systems.

Dunn, V. B. (1985). *Toward a mission statement for interprofessional education and practice: Sanctions, characteristics and assumptions.* Columbus: Commission on Interprofessional Education and Practice.

Falck, H. S. (Spring 1977). Interdisciplinary education and implications for social work practice. *Journal of Education for Social Work, 13*(2), 30–37.

Harbaugh, G. L. (1973). *Death: A theological reformulation of developmental and existential perspectives.* Unpublished doctoral dissertation, University of Chicago.

———. (1976). Paper presented at "Death, Dying, and Other Losses" convocation, Springfield, OH.

———. (Winter 1983). A model for caring. *Thanatos.*

———. (1984a). *Pastor as person.* Minneapolis: Augsburg.

———. (1984b). The person in ministry: Psychological type and the seminary. *Journal of Psychological Type, 8,* 23–32.

———. (1985). Wholeness and helping: Self-reports on interprofessional training, cited in Harbaugh, G. L., Casto, R. M., and Burgess-Ellison, J. A. (1987). Becoming a professional: How interprofessional training helps. *Theory into Practice, 26*(2), 141–145.

———. (1990). *God's gifted people* (expanded ed.). Minneapolis: Augsburg.

———. (1992). *Caring for the caregiver.* Washington, DC: The Alban Institute.

Harbaugh, G. L., Behrens, W. C., Hudson, J., and Oswald, R. (1986). *Beyond the boundary.* Washington, DC: The Alban Institute.

Kane, R. A. (1983). *Interprofessional teamwork.* Syracuse, NY: Syracuse University School of Social Work, Manpower Monograph No. 8.

Medalie, J. H., Kitson, G. C., and Zyzanski, S. J. (1981). A family epidemiological model: A practice and research concept for family medicine. *The Journal of Family Practice, 12*(1), 79–87.

Myers, I. B., with Myers, P. (1980). *Gifts differing.* Palo Alto, CA: Consulting Psychologists Press.

Myers, I. B., and McCaulley, M. H. (1985). *Manual: A guide to the development and use of the Myers-Briggs Type Indicator.* Palo Alto, CA: Consulting Psychologists Press.

Spiegel, J. (1982). An ecological model of ethnic families. In McGoldrick, M., Pearce, J., and Giordano, J. (Eds.), *Ethnicity and Family Therapy.* New York: Guilford Press. 1982.

Tagliaferre, L., and Harbaugh, G. L. (1990). *Recovery from loss.* Deerfield Beach, FL: Health Communications.

CHAPTER 3

Professionalization and Socialization in Interprofessional Collaboration

Wynne R. Waugaman, C.R.N.A., Ph.D.

PROFESSIONALIZATION AND ROLE IDENTITY

Professionalism can mean different things to different people. Professionals are problem-solvers. They are highly educated and trained individuals. All professions have certain minimum criteria and standards required for qualification and maintenance of the professional credential. Professionalism is a way of life, not merely a job (Finniston, 1980, p. 146). Individuals are socialized into professions that possess specific bodies of knowledge, expertise, values, and standards by which the members disseminate information, practice, and abide. Professionalism includes responsibility beyond one's paid hours.

■ Selecting a Profession

Why do people select one profession instead of another for their life's work? Christman (1978, p. 19) believes that most people begin preparing for their chosen careers only vaguely understanding the implications of the career choice. Vollmer and Mills (1966, p. 87) view becoming a professional as a lengthy process that begins long before the individual is accepted into a professional school. In fact, a person's attitudes toward the chosen profession may be rooted in childhood experiences that are later modified, but nonetheless have an impact on the career path chosen (Ducanis and Golin, 1979, p. 25).

A change in personal behavior generally accompanies the acquisition of a profession's body of knowledge. Professional development involves a realization that professionals have ethical and moral responsibilities to their clients. Professional responsibilities extend not only to professionals' own clients and colleagues but to all groups with which professionals interact. Recognition as a profession comes from acknowledgment by all groups with which the profession works as well as by other professions.

■ *Professionalization*

Professionalization, the process of becoming a profession, is evaluated by the degree to which a given profession meets the criteria of the classic professions of law, medicine, and divinity (McCloskey, 1981, p. 40). Although numerous lists of criteria for professions exist in the literature, the recurring themes of knowledge and altruism seem to be consistent. Each profession has its own body of knowledge, skills, and expertise. Often this body of knowledge is measured and compared with that of other professions through professional scholarly writing and publication (Waugaman, 1992, p. 1). For its part, professional altruism ensures that the client is not exploited by the professional's knowledge and skills.

Professions hold autonomy as an ideal. The ability to function freely and independently has been used both for and against groups of "professionals." An occupation that lacks autonomy has no mechanism established for self-direction and more than likely does not have available to it sufficient resources to develop the economic rewards that result from self-direction (Brutvan, 1985, p. 3). Etzioni (1969) described occupations such as teaching, social work, and nursing as semi-professions. Overall, these professions historically seem to have had less control over their own work through educational standards, licensing, and legislation. The autonomy of these groups is changing but does not equal that of the classic or traditional professions (Waugaman, 1993).

Societal changes and value shifts influence the professions and professionalization (McCloskey, 1981, p. 40). Professionalization is a mechanism that promotes social mobility within U.S. society. Demographic and population changes as well as advances in media, communication, and technology all have an impact on the professions. The changing status of women and its impact particularly on the male-dominated traditional professions—such as law, medicine, and divinity—are and will continue to have important effects on professionalism. Relationships among the professions will become more collaborative and less hierarchial (Fagin, 1992, p. 295). The public view of the professions will have an impact on the professional role, particularly within the interprofessional team. In the health care industry, public esteem for physicians has deteriorated, along with the concept of physician omnipotence, while the professional autonomy of and esteem for nurses has risen (Stein, Watts, and Howell, 1990, p. 546).

Sociologically, the development of a profession involves more than developing a distinct body of knowledge. It involves the realization that professionals are part of an ethical and moral community. The helping professions in particular espouse an ethical and moral basis for their professional practice (see Chapter 11). These ethics and mores must be examined in interactions with clients. Ethical issues are illustrated in the case studies found in Chapter 10. Professional ethical dilemmas are demonstrated particularly in the cases of Roger and of Jessica. Professionals have social links not only to their clients and colleagues in the profession, but also to all groups with whose activities their skills must interface. The legitimacy of their professional contribution must be acknowledged by all groups with which they work as well as by other professions.

PROFESSIONAL SOCIALIZATION

Professional education transforms nonprofessionals into professionals through a process known as professional socialization. Professional socialization is a process of developing skills, knowledge, professional behavior, and career commitment, and it occurs concurrently with the education process.

The professional socialization process has been studied in a variety of professions. This process shows commonalities across the professions. Are students really socialized to assume a professional role? Students are shaped both by intent and by unplanned circumstances of their academic environment.

■ *Patterns of Socialization*

One pattern of socialization described by Merton et al. (1957) focuses on professional education itself and the acquisition of the professional role during this process. This pattern considers attitudes, values, and outlook as well as the skills and knowledge that constitute the professional role (Merton, Reader, and Kendall, 1957, p. 287). This pattern of behavior takes motivation for granted and views students as being "inducted" into a professional role.

Another pattern of socialization (Becker et al., 1961) views the school as a social organism or social system. This pattern centers on motivation, identities, and commitments. Social control appears to be a matter of power. Behavioral options increase power; constraints on behavior reduce it. These constraints put pressure on students to limit their ability to act in accordance with their goals

(Becker et al., 1961) in order to achieve a sense of well-being and comfort (Olesen and Whittaker, 1968). This view of socialization sees learning as situational; previous ways of dealing with problems are unlikely to be adaptable when the conditions change (Becker et al., 1961).

The main difference between these two views of professional socialization centers on the question of social control of behavior—its place and its effects on the orientation and behavior of the student and the professional (Simpson, 1979). The model proposed by Merton et al. (1957) pictures a profession as a group with a unity of purpose, with social control of the members arising from shared outlooks and mutual interests. The professional school is conceived as both a part and an instrument of a profession, charged with the responsibility of inducting students into the profession in a way that ensures its continuous structure. Students learn the accepted behaviors and professional moral and ethical values that guide them as professionals to act in ways consistent with the professional role. According to Becker et al. (1961), in contrast, a professional product is not produced during professional education.

■ Impact of Socialization

Professional socialization is a directional change or pattern of changes that adjusts students to their professional roles; but unlike adjustments to specific situations, professional socialization persists. It persists across status transitions and situational changes; thus socialization endures over time and space. According to Simpson (1979) and Waugaman (1988), professional socialization encompasses not only occupational knowledge and skills but occupational orientations such as collegialism, a preference for working within the institutional organizational structure, and views concerning leadership and authority (see Table 3.1). Task-centered problem-solving seems to be inherent within the helping professions. This type of problem-solving is exemplified in the cases of Olga and S.B.

Socialization also enables the student to form a personal relatedness to the field through developing career commitment and self-identification in the role to which he or she aspires. Simpson (1979) proposes a view of socialization in which dimensions of the socialization process are differentiated. This view of socialization seems to overcome the oversocialized view of workers implicit in the model proposed by Merton et al. (1957) as well as to help overcome the limitations of the model of social control proposed by Becker et al. (1961).

The socialization process is dynamic. An individual's view of the professional role may shift to fit the circumstances and demands of a work situation without any effect on job commitment (Simpson, 1979, p. 45). On the other hand, with changing family, social roles, and social orientations, commitment to the job itself may decline while views of the work role and the professional occupation remain stable. This is the ever-changing face of professional socialization. Professional roles adapt as necessary to suit the situation.

TABLE 3.1 ■
The Dimensions of Socialization

DIMENSION	DEFINITION
Education	The imparting of occupational knowledge and skill in a profession
Cognitive occupational orientations	
Cognitive orientations to the occupational role	Orientation to the functions of the professional role, e.g. nurse
Cognitive orientations to a place in the occupation	Expressing the interests of the professional organization and the professional position within the field (such as the position of medicine or nursing within the health care industry)
Relatedness to the professional role	The individual is related to the chosen profession in three ways: status identification through socioeconomic rewards, personal attraction to the profession, and commitment to the chosen career

■ *Socialization and Education*

Early exposure to practicum and learning the work of the profession facilitate all aspects of professional socialization, particularly in the traditional professions (Waugaman, 1988, p. 3). Role modeling by mentors and faculty in an education program is a valuable tool of professional socialization. Throughout the mentoring process, students learn the professional language, behavior, and conceptual framework of the chosen profession. Although the inculcation of these professional characteristics and values into professional behavior enhances communication within the intraprofessional team, it may create misperceptions and conflict between professionals in an interprofessional team who have been socialized differently.

The emphasis in some professions' education on practical experience during the curriculum enables students to visualize their professional roles with a high degree of realism from an early point in the educational process. Practical experience thus may facilitate socialization into the chosen profession. Educational program content and design and faculty, practitioner, and mentor role models all play a vital role in professional socialization (Waugaman, 1994, p. 16). All these factors influence the degree to which students are socialized into the profession. The continuation of this socialization process influences the degree of professional career commitment as individuals mature within their chosen professions. This process may change over time but continues throughout professional careers and has an impact on the way individuals deal with situations and interact with other professionals.

INTERPROFESSIONAL SOCIALIZATION

Professional socialization is the process by which nonmembers are exposed to certain experiences regarded by members of the profession as necessary for gaining inclusion into the profession. Upon completion of this period, the individual is accorded membership, with rights, privileges, and status as a publicly identified member of the group (Mizrahi, 1986, p. 21). Included in this process is learning what defines a group member (Hadden and Long, 1978). This professional process sets the stage for success in effective communications and problem-solving in interprofessional collaboration.

Interprofessional socialization must occur for effective teamwork, since professions do not operate in a vacuum. Interprofessional socialization is a convergent process, where team professional goals move toward a common point. In contrast, intraprofessional socialization is divergent, where each individual's goals may move in different directions from a common professional starting point. Professionals must be socialized to interact and communicate in collaboration with one another. Interprofessional collaboration was defined in Chapter 2, but it goes without saying that problem-solving for a given client is the common professional goal. Each professional brings to the interprofessional team not only his or her own set of professional norms and values, but knowledge, expertise, skills, and autonomy. All professionals know what is expected from them in their professional roles. However, as mentioned in Chapter 1, professionals are truly not taught within their own professions to work in teams with members of other disciplines.

Although certain aspects of professionalism, such as peer review of work, appear to militate toward equality among all disciplines, in interprofessional teamwork not all professionals within a bureaucracy may be permitted to function at the same optimum professional level. Changing team roles and shifts in team leadership have been alluded to earlier in this chapter and will be discussed more fully in Chapter 5. In spite of the movement toward flexibility in team roles to best meet client needs, in certain traditional teams, one team member remains the leader or the "super consultant," such as the physician in health care teams (Brody, 1976; Schuman et al., 1976; Zola and Miller, 1973).

Physicians often have difficulty in dealing with these changing roles. They are puzzled and confused by those who do not automatically confer the team leader role upon them (Stein, Watts, and Howell, 1990, p. 549). Under stress or conflict in the group, a physician may tend to pull away from the group. This tendency more than likely results from the fact that physicians, more than other professionals, have not traditionally been taught or socialized into the collaborative model of work (Kurtz, 1980, p. 34). In fact, the collaborative model may be the complete opposite of the way physicians are socialized to solve problems.

■ *Application of Interprofessional Socialization*

Comprehensive care today requires the broad spectrum of knowledge that no one professional can provide. We face problems today that are so complex that only a multidisciplinary approach can be effective. As illustrated in some of the case studies in Chapter 10, AIDS, domestic violence, substance abuse, homelessness, the aging population, and Alzheimer's disease are only a few of the problems facing society today (Mariano, 1989, p. 285). Collaboration has reduced health care costs and has often increased quality of care (Fagin, 1992, p. 297).

For collaboration to be effective, all professionals must be educated interdisciplinarily. Collaborative models must be discussed in the classroom and practiced in the clinical laboratory. Only through educational reform and changes in professional socialization will interprofessional collaboration truly become effective as a model of care. We have become a nation of professionals who specialize. We tend to see things in a fragmentary way, according to our respective specialties, rather than holistically. Collaboration involves combining efforts and sharing professional assets to provide a broader spectrum of information that can become a comprehensive plan to meet the needs of the client (Trueman, 1991, p. 70).

Collaborative practice is not designed or dictated by management or any single professional; rather, it is managed by all team professionals, who share responsibility for the client's outcomes. Interprofessional socialization must occur for all professionals to interact more effectively. This process enables the team to seek a unified direction for problem-solving through commitment to achieving common goals and objectives in order to arrive at an integrated outcome.

SUMMARY

Professionals must become socialized into their roles in order to acquire the skills, knowledge, professional behavior, and commitment inherent to their chosen professions. The profession in which one gains membership is valued by all professions for its distinct body of knowledge and its contributions to society. One aspect of professional development is the professional's assumption of ethical and moral responsibilities toward clients and colleagues. Part of the professional socialization process must enable professionals to work effectively with colleagues from other professions through collaboration.

Traditionally, not all professions have espoused the interprofessional collaborative model. However, as the problems we face today become more complex, we must be prepared to work collaboratively with many professionals to achieve the optimum outcome for clients. The achievement of interprofessional collaboration in client care will demand the cooperation of all professions in educational reform and interprofessional socialization.

REFERENCES AND RELATED READINGS

Abramson, J., and Mizrahi, T. (1986). Strategies for enhancing collaboration between social workers and physicians. *Social Work in Health Care, 12,* 1–21.

Becker, H., Hughes, E., et al. (1961). *Boys in white.* Chicago: University of Chicago Press.

Brody, S. (1976). A diagnostic and treatment center for the aging: A program of preplacement intervention. *The Gerontologist, 16,* 47–51.

Brutvan, E. L. (1985). Intra-role conflict: A result of naive attempts toward professionalization. *Journal of Allied Health, 14,* 3–11.

Christman, L. (1978). Educational standards versus professional performance. *Nursing Digest, 6,* 27–44.

Cohen, H. (1980). Authoritarianism and dependency: Problems in nursing socialization. In Flynn, B., and Miller, M. (Eds.), *Current perspectives in nursing: Social issues and trends.* St. Louis: C.V. Mosby.

Ducanis, A. J., and Golin, A. K. (1979). *The interdisciplinary health care team.* Germantown, MD: Aspen Systems.

Etzioni, A. (Ed). (1969). *The semi-professions and their organization.* New York: Free Press.

Fagin, C. M. (1992). Collaboration between nurses and physicians: No longer a choice. *Academic Medicine, 67*(5), 295–303.

Finniston, M. (1980). Professionalism: A way of life. *British Dental Journal, 149,* 143–146.

Hadden, J., and Long, T. (1978). *A study of physician socialization.* Report to the U.S. Department of Health, Education, and Welfare.

Hardy, L. K. (1984). The emergence of nursing leaders—A case of in spite of, not because of. *International Nursing Review, 31,* 11–15.

Kurtz, M. E. A. (1980). A behavioral profile of physicians in management roles. In Schonke, R. (Ed.), *Physicians in management.* Tampa, FL: American Academy of Medical Directors.

Lurie, E. E. (1981). Nurse practitioners: Issues in professional socialization. *Journal of Health and Social Behavior, 22,* 31–48.

Mariano, C. (1989). The case for interdisciplinary collaboration. *Nursing Outlook, 37*(6), 285–288.

McCloskey, J. C. (1981). The professionalization of nursing: United States and England. *International Nursing Review, 28,* 40–47.

Merton, R., Reader, G., and Kendall, P. (1957). *The student physician.* Cambridge, MA: Harvard University Press.

Mizrahi, T. (1986). *Getting rid of patients: Contradictions in the socialization of physicians.* New Brunswick, NJ: Rutgers University Press.

Olesen, V. L., and Whittaker, E. W. (1968). *The silent dialogue.* San Francisco: Jossey-Bass.

Schuman, J., Ostfeld, A., and Willard, H. (1976). Discharge planning in an acute hospital. *Archives of Physical Medicine and Rehabilitation, 57,* 343–347.

Simpson, I. H. (1979). *From student to nurse.* New York: Cambridge University Press.

Stein, L. I., Watts, D. T., and Howell, T. (1990). The doctor–nurse game revisited. *New England Journal of Medicine, 322,* 546–549.

Tisher, R. P. (1979). *Teacher induction: An aspect of the education and professional development of teachers.* Paper presented at the National Invitational Conference "Exploring Issues in Teacher Education: Questions for Future Research," Austin, TX.

Trueman, M. S. (1991). Collaboration: A right and responsibility of professional practice. *Critical Care Nurse, 11*(1), 70–72.

Vollmer, H. M., and Mills, D. L. (Eds.). (1966). *Professionalization.* Englewood Cliffs, NJ: Prentice-Hall.

Waugaman, W. R. (1988). From nurse to nurse anesthetist. In Waugaman, W. R., et al. (Eds.), *Principles and practice of nurse anesthesia* (1st ed.). East Norwalk, CT: Appleton and Lange.

————. (1992). Publication as a measure of professionalism. *Nurse Anesthesia, 3,* 1–3.

————. (1994). Professional roles of the CRNA. In Foster, S., and Jordan, L. (Eds.), *Professional issues in nurse anesthesia practice.* Philadelphia: F.A. Davis.

Zola, J., and Miller, S. (1973). The erosion of medicine from within. In Freidson, E. (Ed.), *The professions and their prospects.* Beverly Hills: Sage.

PART 2

A Way of Understanding
The Processes of
Interprofessional Care
and
Collaborative Practice

CHAPTER 4

Group Process
and
Interprofessional Teamwork

María C. Juliá, M.S.W., Ph.D.
Arlene Thompson, R.N., Ph.D.

OVERVIEW: HISTORY OF TEAMWORK IN THE HELPING PROFESSIONS

Teamwork in the helping professions is not new. A study of the word *team* over time reveals an evolution in meaning (Schmitt, 1982). Initially, *team* implied a group based on likeness that combined similar efforts to obtain a goal. As specialization occurred, it became evident that some activities could be accomplished better by a specialized division of labor. Thus, *team* came to mean a group comprising different parts coming together to achieve a common goal. Early references to teams, however, were related to single professions. Barker (1922), for instance, suggested that teamwork in health care practice was needed to bring together medical specialists who could draw on their different knowledge and skills to bring the best medical knowledge to bear on patient problems.

Multiprofessional teams, those that represented more than one profession, began to appear in the 1940s (Schmitt, 1982). Special areas of chronic illness and rehabilitation recognized the need to address the complexities of the total health needs, not only the presenting physical problems. Multidisciplinary teams became a common phenomenon in the health care field in the 1960s and were composed of representatives from a variety of professions, including medicine, nursing, social work, vocational education, physical therapy, occupational therapy, nutrition, and other health care fields.

It has only been since the early 1970s that interprofessional teamwork has emerged. The interprofessional team differs from single professional and multi-professional teams in that it "involves the interaction of various disciplines around an agreed-upon goal to be achieved only through a complex integration or synthesis of various disciplinary perspectives" (Schmitt, 1982, p. 183). In health care practice, for example, the goals have broadened to include a focus on health and quality of life, not merely on the resolution of medical problems.

While the phenomenon of teamwork was emerging in the health fields, a number of disciplines began to give attention to the study and understanding of how and why groups work. Numerous theoretical frameworks were developed to provide a sound, logical approach to the study and understanding of groups (Phipps, 1982). Major contributions in this direction have come from the disciplines of psychiatry, psychology, communication, sociology, social work, and education. Important literature on the advancement of group work over the past 70 years has come from pioneers such as Joseph Pratt, Trignant Burrow, Jacob Moreno, Kurt Lewin, Abraham Maslow, M. A. Lieberman, and I. D. Yalom (Moreno, 1951; Lewin, 1951; Lieberman et al., 1973; Yalom, 1975).

Two events are noteworthy in the discussion of applied theory of group work (Janosik and Phipps, 1982). The first, the Northfield experiment, occurred as the direct result of the stresses and demands of World War II. Because of the large numbers of battle-fatigued and emotional casualties of the war, a group of physicians in Northfield, England, suspended army protocol and treated military patients in small groups, like civilians. Foulkes, a psychiatrist, proposed the idea that a person's network of personal relationships during an illness had a profound effect on recovery (Anthony, 1971); the small groups provided the community network that was thought to promote the restoration of health. The Northfield experiment provided much of the impetus for the development of group theory following the war (Phipps, 1982).

The second important development that significantly influenced the development of group work theory was the creation in 1947 of the National Training Laboratory for Applied Behavioral Science in Bethel, Maine. As a number of helping professions began to apply the theory of group work in the care of clients, industry and government saw the advantages of understanding the ways groups function. Consequently, much of the funding for the National Training Laboratory came from government and private industry. The goal of teaching group dynamics to those in managerial and executive positions was to increase awareness of the manager's influence on interaction in a group. Other objectives of the educational training groups were to increase understanding of group dynamics, increase competency in handling difficult situations, and relate these ideas to effectiveness in job performance (Anthony, 1971).

The study of group behavior has produced important information about the function and process of groups. Effective interprofessional teamwork that produces significant outcomes occurs when knowledge about group theory and interprofessional collaboration is applied to the team process.

BASIC ASSUMPTIONS ABOUT GROUP PROCESSES

To examine the interprofessional team, basic assumptions about group process need to be stated. "There are many ways of looking at anything so complex as group process" (Odhner, 1970, p. 486), and the extensive body of literature on the subject makes the topic of group process theories beyond the scope of this chapter.[1] Those preparing professional students for interdisciplinary practice, however, must be concerned with enhancing competence in elements of small group process. The following working assumptions make the necessity for this competence clear.

1. The interprofessional team is a small group subject to the same laws that govern any primary group; the professionals' behavior on an interprofessional team is a product of group process (Kane, 1976).
2. To be an effective team member, one must have knowledge about and skills in the group processes that underlie the interaction of team members and accept group processes as part of effective interprofessional team functioning (Germain, 1984).
3. The appropriate utilization of the interprofessional team approach and the successful achievement of desired outcomes depend on the cognitive grasp, sensitive understanding, and careful handling of a number of specific dynamics conceptually grouped under the generic label of interprofessional group process (Billups, 1987).

Interprofessional team process comprises "purposeful sequences of change-oriented transactions between representatives of two or more professions who possess individual expertise, but who are functionally interdependent in their collaborative pursuit of commonly shared goals" (Billups, 1987). As this author points out, interprofessional team process consists not of one process but of a series of subprocesses, which probably take place simultaneously instead of in sequence.

What process theory attempts to describe is the dynamic interaction or the relationships involved among the unique parts of a whole. Process theory involves the recognition and assessment of a pattern of functioning. When we look at process, we are involved in a "reflective appraisal" of a situation: completed actions are reflected upon and evaluated (Lowe and Herramen,

---

[1] For the reader interested in further study of group process theories, the bibliography includes a selection of classic resources on the topic.

1978), allowing us to see where the group is heading, available alternatives, the consequences of actions, and how members feel about the actions taken.

GROUP LIFE: DEVELOPMENTAL STAGES OF A GROUP

Groups are not static. Just as one can describe the growth and development stages of a person's life, so can stages of a group's existence be identified. Three stages can be identified in the life of a group over time. Several authors have defined those stages as the initial, middle, and final stages, each having specific characteristics (Janosik and Phipps, 1982; Loomis, 1979; Marram, 1978).

Brill, however, identifies five stages in the evolution of a team, each with characteristics, tasks, and outcomes (1976). The first stage is the orientation stage, in which members in a group determine their position with reference to setting and circumstances. In this stage, members begin to define the situation and clarify the group's purpose. Each member is intent on learning what is expected in the group and relates what he or she learns to his or her self-perception. This clarification occurs through interaction among members and with the leader. Also at this time, individual members, who are often unfamiliar with other group members, deal with the stress and anxiety of a new situation. The team's tasks in the orientation stage are twofold. The first task is to define the group's boundaries and to clarify the group's purpose and tasks. The second orientation task of the team members is to provide support to one another. As this stage progresses, members become acquainted with one another, understanding of the task and expectations of the group become clearer, an initial sense of security within the group develops, and a beginning involvement and identification with other group members takes place.

The second stage in the development of the group or team is the accommodation stage. This stage involves a process of adaptation and arrangement to create a whole entity. Characteristics at this stage of the group's life include manipulation among members and movement and change of positions within the group; also, power struggles may sometimes emerge during this stage. The major task of the individual group members at this time is to find an appropriate place for themselves within the group. This process of positioning oneself occurs on both a personal and a professional level. The team task in this stage is to provide structure and a climate conducive to maximum freedom for members. The outcomes of this stage are the emergence of a common language and a pattern of communication that elicits understanding among group members. The values and norms of the group are developing. Attitudinal affiliation and cohesiveness begin to emerge.

A third stage identified by Brill is the negotiation phase, during which a mutual understanding is evident in the group's team characteristics, including the establishment of boundaries and the content of members' specialization in relation to other members (1976). Overlapping roles are worked out, areas of specialization are identified, and the bargaining process among members concludes. The team members become comfortable in their roles and are able to communicate, differ, confront, use conflict, and promote collaboration with one another. At this time the team as a group defines the boundaries of its purpose, establishes a contract among the members, and designates the goals, tasks, and roles that will be assumed. Unity develops and areas of differentiation are established.

The fourth stage is known as the operation stage. During this time purposeful action of the team is observed. Complementary role function is achieved, and a sense of the whole emerges. Members of the team are able to relate to the team as a whole and to individual members of the team. In this phase, team members use both generalized information and specialized knowledge in order to reach individual decisions and perform tasks necessary to reach team goals. The team as a unit is very active at this stage. Both internal and external balance are maintained, and the team's vitality reflects the energy generated within the group. Active decision-making occurs, along with the planning and execution of work. The outcome is collaborative movement toward achieving goals and realizing the purpose of the team. The operation stage is essential to achieve the desired goals established in the early development of the group.

The fifth and final stage is one of dissolution, when the cohesive group begins the process of separation into its original components. The team's tasks have been accomplished, and evaluation takes place. Areas included in the evaluation are assessment of the process that took place, identification of problems that emerged, and discussion of achievement in relation to the team's purpose and stated goals. At this time, team members assess their personal and team performance. The team as a whole supports open and critical evaluation of the team's process and results. A primary outcome of this stage is awareness of the group's success and failure. Personal and team change is identified. Closure is made among members. It is not uncommon for teams to avoid the final stage because of the uneasiness that often accompanies termination. However, each stage is important in team functioning, and each stage has a significant outcome for the team member. Avoidance of closure activities leaves the group in an unresolved state and inhibits the final process of termination.

Other authors, such as Lowe and Herramen (1981) and Kane (1976), set out conceptual variations on the stages just presented but basically cover the same phenomena. Although the stages may be described in different ways and in different orders, the developmental process of group life is predictable. The stages through which an interprofessional team progresses produce an expanded level of thinking that is not possible in multiprofessional or single-professional teams. The analysis and synthesis of thought that takes place in the interprofessional group is an outcome greater than the sum of the parts that make up the team. This expanded level of thinking is the unique and desired outcome of interprofessional teamwork.

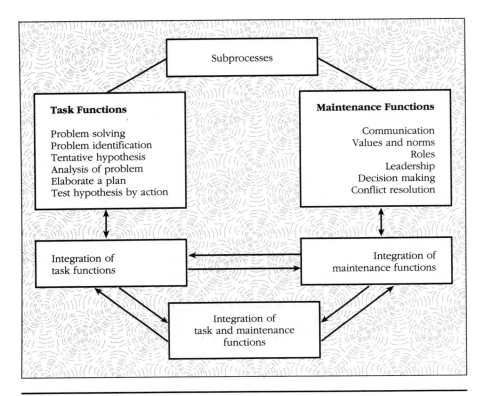

FIGURE 4.1 ■
Interprofessional team process

INTERPROFESSIONAL TEAM PROCESSES

The productivity of an interprofessional group depends on an aspect of collaboration that many teams fail to recognize and deal with, the group process. Therefore, our intention in Chapter 5 is to introduce and sensitize the reader to a selected number of process variables. How the process work actually gets done seems to be the heart of the matter in teamwork (Horwitz, 1970). Put simply, process is a way or method of doing something; it has been conceptualized as "the recurrent patterning of changes over time and in a particular direction" (Holfstein, 1964).

Figure 4.1 illustrates the interprofessional team process elements that will be discussed in the next chapter. As Figure 4.1 depicts, teams (and interprofessional teams in particular) integrate differentiated functions—task and maintenance functions—that are considered related and complementary (Germain, 1984). Team collaboration is essentially a problem-solving process, and the "ideal team" is one that is continually in the process of evaluating and improving its task and maintenance functions throughout every stage of its life (Hooyman, 1984).

Task functions, listed on the left side of Figure 4.1, parallel the steps involved in the problem-solving process, encompassing activities such as problem identification, development of a tentative hypothesis, analysis of the situation, elaboration and implementation of a plan, and evaluation. These task functions are integrated, and although they are presented in a list in Figure 4.1, they should be thought of as a set of interacting elements affecting one another. The same type of interaction takes place among the maintenance functions listed on the right side of Figure 4.1. Maintenance and task processes and activities essential to effective team functioning affect one another as illustrated by the arrows connecting both sides of the figure. According to Hooyman, achieving an appropriate balance of task and maintenance functions is the most crucial aspect of team functioning (1984). "The effectiveness and productivity of any group in any setting is related to both its capabilities to do the work and its ability to manage itself as an interdependent group of people" (Rubin and Beckhard, 1972, p. 1317).

The following chapter discusses those interdependent tasks and maintenance functions that occur simultaneously and are the basic elements of group process in the interprofessional team. The bibliography for this chapter has been combined with that for Chapter 5 and can be found at the conclusion of that chapter.

Essential Elements of Interprofessional Teamwork
Task and Maintenance Functions

María C. Juliá, M.S.W., Ph.D.

Arlene Thompson, R.N., Ph.D.

This chapter elaborates on the task and maintenance functions of interprofessional teams introduced in Chapter 4. Without attention to and effective integration of these essential functions, interprofessional collaboration would not be possible.

TASK FUNCTIONS

Interprofessional teams, as distinct from other types of teams, are primarily task oriented. They essentially use a problem-solving model, following a systematic approach to fulfill collectively agreed-on goals—an approach referred to as the task oriented process. In completing a task, it is essential for the interprofessional team member to be aware of the problem-solving process and the sub-processes it comprises: problem identification, development of a tentative hypothesis, analysis of the problem, elaboration of a plan, and testing the hypothesis through action.

Team task behavior comprises the content of the team discussion and the methods that accomplish the team's task. The task is the team's reason for being—the purpose for which it was formed. In the interprofessional team, one can assume that the purpose has already been determined by a force outside the team itself—the external force instrumental to the team's formation. Thus, in the initial stages of team life, the primary issue facing the team is the clarification of an established task, not the determination of the team's purpose.

Because the team exists to accomplish a predetermined task, certain characteristics of team functioning will hold. First, the boundaries of an interprofessional team are open and must remain open to the external environment, because external factors sanction and give purpose to the team. For example, an academic faculty team that plans and teaches an interprofessional course in a university or in a geriatric evaluation unit of a hospital is given organizational sanction to meet. The team is expected to accomplish the task of providing student instruction or patient care, respectively. Team existence and team task accomplishment depend on support from the formal organizational structure and the existence of unmet needs on the part of a service recipient. For another example, a community-based interprofessional team is a team formed by individuals who represent community agencies or private practice. This informal organization similarly has team boundaries that are and must remain open to the community forces that sanction the existence of an interprofessional team for the delivery of human services.

Second, the outcome of team behavior that will be of primary interest both to those in the outside environment and to the individual team members is a specific, concrete product that fulfills the requirement of task completion. The outcome evidence of task completion will be some type of service intervention for the recipient.

The process by which an effective interprofessional team accomplishes a task includes a problem-solving orientation. The nature of an interprofessional team approach to task accomplishment, however, is embedded in the intellectual authority inherent in professional problem-solving. It can be argued, then, that the content and the process of interprofessional team functioning both consist of ideas.

■ Problem-Solving Orientation

The interprofessional team in the delivery of human services is a composite of unique and distinct professional orientations brought together to solve a variety of human problems. These many and varied professional orientations provide alternative views of the nature of the human problems in the situation at hand and the services required to resolve them. The multiple orientations represented in an interprofessional team increase the possibility that the wholeness of the person being served will be better comprehended and that the problem will be more completely described and analyzed.

The use of knowledge by and intellectual development of the professions are important to consider as factors that affect the interprofessional team. A profession also develops a sociological orientation in addition to a distinct body of knowledge, as Waugaman suggests (see Chapter 3 for a complete discussion of this topic). Two important aspects of a professional orientation to problem-solving, therefore, are a professional's distinct body of knowledge and a professional's particular problem-solving process. These are inherent to what it means to be a professional. Each of these characteristics will be identified and discussed to demonstrate how they affect both task and maintenance functions in the interprofessional team process.

The first characteristic of a profession is that each profession has a unique, identifiable body of knowledge. The knowledge base of each profession provides the intellectual authority for practice. The formulation and articulation of ideas and practice-based experience from which the profession draws its authority are the responsibility of those within the profession. This theoretical and practical authority give rise to the domain of inquiry and practice of the professional and provide the boundaries and rules for practitioners' behavior as professionals. Each member of a profession has both the right and the ultimate responsibility to argue the truth and usefulness of ideas within his or her professional domain. Those who are outside the profession may challenge and critique the domain of inquiry, but the ultimate responsibility for that domain resides within each profession.

The intellectual authority of the profession may be an issue in the interprofessional team. The tension among professionals in an interprofessional team may in part be explained by the areas of uncertainty within each profession's body of knowledge and the overlap among professions that derive their intellectual authority from the same discipline. For example, a physician, a social worker, a nurse, a teacher, an occupational therapist, and a minister all derive a knowledge base for individual behavior from the discipline of psychology. Within the discipline of psychology there are several schools of thought to explain how or why people behave as they do. The tension that naturally surrounds the uncertainty of knowledge about individual behavior will provide a source of conflict among professionals discussing a single case. When the interprofessional team deliberates to identify problems and develop collaborative plans to resolve the problems in an individual case, team members will draw from the knowledge base of their individual professions. The maintenance of an honest intellectual discourse to preserve the intellectual integrity of the professional is required for effective interprofessional problem-solving.

A second characteristic of professions that affects the interprofessional team is each profession's unique problem-solving process. The education of the professional includes developing a method of thinking and the ability to apply correctly the knowledge required to practice as a professional. During their education, professionals are taught a systematic approach for handling practical situations they might encounter and how to think as professionals in those situations. Professionals refer to this systematic approach to the problem situation in different ways—for example, the scientific method, the case study method, the problem-solving process, or developing a plan of action. Professionals' orientation to a problem situation, though given different names, has a common characteristic—that is, it is a disciplined approach to thinking about the situation when developing a professional plan of action to resolve the problems encountered in the situation.

These two characteristics of a professional—the possession of a distinct body of knowledge and the use of a unique problem-solving process—often lead to unjustified criticism of turf protection among professionals, which militates against effective interprofessional collaboration. Professionals' knowledge claims and distinct methods of solving practice problems may set up barriers to interprofessional communication. Communication problems may also arise from lack of a common professional language; this barrier has led to the development of instructional strategies to teach interprofessional communication. Describing one's profession in a team discussion provides the opportunity to reduce role stereotyping and increase understanding of one another's professions. Instructional strategies designed to develop a common professional language derived from existing professions will yield greater mutual understanding and respect for different professions' strengths, commitments and uniqueness.

Professional problem-solving models provide a common professional language to resolve this communication problem among professionals in collaboration. The same intellectual method of systematic thinking provides a common language that is central to interprofessional communication and collaboration. The professional language offers a common basis from which a collaborative plan can emerge. Though the words used to describe the method may vary, the method itself is the same for all professionals.

■ *Reflective Intelligence*[1]

The work of the educational philosopher John Dewey supports the idea of a common professional language just discussed (1904). He observed the intellectual method that professionals in law, medicine, and engineering used to solve practical problems. His concept of reflective intelligence describes how people think before taking action when resolving problems. The general process of reflective intelligence, or the reflective experience, is as follows:

1. Perplexity, confusion, and doubt resulting from one's implication in an incomplete situation, the full character of which is not yet determined.
2. A conjectural anticipation or a tentative interpretation of given elements, attributing to them a tendency to certain consequences.

[1] The authors would like to acknowledge the contributions of Eleanor Nystrom, Ph.D., during the initial stages of preparation of this chapter.

3. A careful survey (examination, inspection, exploration, analysis) of all attainable considerations that will define and clarify the problem at hand.
4. A consequent elaboration of the tentative hypothesis to make it more precise and more consistent by squaring with a wider range of facts.
5. Taking a stand on the projected hypothesis by drawing up a plan of action that is then applied to the existing state of affairs—that is, doing something overtly to bring about the anticipated result, thereby testing the hypothesis (Dewey, 1916, p. 150).

The reflective experience Dewey described is similar to the thoughtful inquiry that an interprofessional team must carry out in order to collaborate systematically on a plan of action to address a problem situation. Each team member has the capacity to engage in systematic inquiry, drawing from a unique point of view based on knowledge of his or her own profession. Participation in reflective thinking, in the interprofessional problem-solving approach, is the responsibility of each member of the team. The action the team takes to implement the plan is the emergent product of reflective intelligence. The developed outcome of the plan to solve the identified problem can be studied to evaluate the task effectiveness of the team.

Both dimensions of the problem-solving approach—the intellectual integrity and reflective experience of each profession—must be understood by each professional because of their effect on team function. The interprofessional team must maintain intellectual integrity and must also rely on thinking (the reflective experience) to develop a collaborative plan of action. Necessary conditions to sustain both task and maintenance processes for optimal team function rely on both thinking and feeling. Maintenance functions rely on social-emotional expressions of team members—the ability to communicate how and what each team member feels. Task functions for the interprofessional team rely on what each member knows and how each member thinks about what he or she knows. The natural tension in team behavior between task and maintenance functions occurs when the interprofessional team focuses primarily on task functions, relying on thinking and intellectual integrity to accomplish the task.

MAINTENANCE FUNCTIONS

Interprofessional teams are actually an "integration of differentiated functions" (Pepper, 1984). Dynamics of team processes include both what a team does (the task processes), and how the team members interact (the maintenance processes). In other words, in addition to task-related functions, the team also has functions related to the harmonious and smooth functioning of the team. These maintenance functions are not always recognized, and failure to deal openly with them can cause problems in team interaction and, consequently, in the successful completion of the team task: "too much teamwork fails because of our unwillingness to bring substantive issues to the forefront and consider only the functional rationalities" (New, 1968, p. 332).

VARIABLES IN TEAM PROCESS

With any phenomenon that is studied, the model, theory, framework, or perspective the professional chooses to use will dictate the variables he or she will utilize. To understand and analyze teamwork, one needs to draw on theoretical constructs from a considerable number of disciplines (Lowe and Herramen, 1981; Horwitz, 1970). Kane warns, however, of the "morass of variables" in which one can get "bogged down" if these variables are not pared down to a small manageable number (1976). She recommends that process elements be consolidated to identify what makes teamwork successful. For interprofessional team process, the selected variables[2] that most affect the process of interaction and team functioning are communication, values and norms, roles, leadership, decision-making, and conflict resolution (see Figure 4.1 on page 40).

■ *Communication*

Communication is the basis for all team functioning. "The very existence of a team depends upon communication, upon exchanging information and upon transmitting meaning" (Johnson and Johnson, 1975, p. 109). The nature of interpersonal communication is complex and the reader is referred to other references for an in-depth discussion. Essentially, communication is a system of concepts that includes a sender, a receiver, a message, a channel for the message, and noise. Noise is any element that interferes with the communication process anywhere in the system. Elements such as the internal encoding and decoding by sender and receiver, or problems in the message or the channel, are sources of noise that interfere with effective interpersonal communication (Johnson and Johnson, 1975, pp. 110–111).

Interpersonal communication among the individuals in a group is basic to interprofessional team function. The team is bound by the rules of communication that lead to effective interpersonal communication. Given the definition of communication as a system of concepts, interprofessional team communication does not differ from interpersonal communication in other groups. Interprofessional team communication differs from that of other teams, however, in the degree to which some professional team members are more skillful and

[2] The reader should be aware of the fact that different authors use different terminology and constructs to describe much the same group process phenomenon. For example, Hooyman (1984) talks about team dynamics; Kane (1976) discusses various components or process elements; Lowe and Herramen (1981) refer to characteristics influencing team functioning.

more alert to the communication process in team function. For example, as part of their professional preparation, nurses, social workers, and occupational therapists study the role of interpersonal communication in the therapeutic context. Because of that orientation, those team members may be more sensitive to and more comfortable with analysis and discussion of the interprofessional team's communication process. Depending on the professional orientation of its members, an interprofessional team thus may have as members individuals who can provide expertise in maintaining effective communication as a team maintenance function. This is not to say other professionals in the team may not be effective communicators. Some team members, however, by virtue of their professional activity may assume greater responsibility for effective interpersonal communication for their interprofessional team.

■ Values and Norms

Brill defines values as "formulations for standards of worth held by both individuals and teams. They presuppose an evaluation or judgment of that which is 'good' or 'bad'; i.e., of greater or lesser worth" (1976, pp. 62–63). Values are also "culturally determined through the process of socialization" (Brill, 1976, p. 63). The values professionals acquire through professional socialization, as well as the personal values held by each professional, affect the interprofessional team (see Chapter 3). As is true of norms, the values held by the team or the professionals involved may be explicit or implicit.

Norms are defined as "attitudes and behaviors that are expected of a person in a certain role in a certain team, or of a certain team in a certain situation" (Brill, 1976, p. 63). Norms carrying the implication of authority affect all aspects of team life and essentially state: "This is how our team works. This is how members behave." Further, because the interprofessional group will necessarily encounter the intellectual authority of each profession in engaging in the team task, the team will experience conflict arising from differences in professional authority, professional values, and professional norms. Because of the conflicts implicit in the differing professional norms and values that exist in the interprofessional team, the team may experience difficulty in discussing the value questions embedded in an interprofessional plan of intervention.

■ Roles

Members of a team assume roles that typify the different positions and various levels of status people hold in a social system. "The statuses are defined in part by both the privileges and obligations that society attaches to them" (Lister, 1982, p. 20). For the team conceptualized as a social system, Bales describes two kinds of roles: task and maintenance roles. The concept of role applied to team process provides a way for team members to characterize the participation of every other member in a team. Norms are ascribed to characterizations, according to the ways members behave in teams. Task and maintenance roles assumed by the members are characterized to assess the degree to which individual participation either facilitates or hinders team process.

In addition to task and maintenance roles, Lister classifies roles in the interprofessional team into personal roles and professional roles (1982). Personal roles based on demographic factors include sex roles, ethnic and cultural roles, and socioeconomic roles. Personal roles depict the person as a human being first, and then as a professional. Each person has a personality preference, a preferred way of perceiving and judging the world (Harbaugh et al., 1987). The personal role a professional plays on the interprofessional team, the expression of one's person, is best understood and appreciated through personality type, gender, ethnocultural history, and socioeconomic status. Personal roles carry different levels of status in the team's social system, and the varying personality types represented by people on the team affect the function of the interprofessional team.

The professional role of each member of the interprofessional team adds another dimension to team life. Professional roles derive from the occupational status of the profession in the larger social system; thus, varying levels of status among the members of the interprofessional team will also be seen by virtue of the occupational groups represented in the interprofessional team. Functional roles such as that of team leader may be expected or assumed by certain professionals based on the occupational status of the professional role. For example, society gives certain rights and responsibilities to physicians through legal regulations and traditions within society. The physician, by virtue of his or her status as a physician, may assume the team leadership function in any team that has no other physician. Yet the other professionals, the interprofessional team, may not see the team leader role as a necessary attribute of the physician status (Lister, 1982, p. 20). Professionals may assume other team function roles based on either professional or personal roles, further complicating the analysis of team role function typically seen in team behavior.

■ *Leadership*

The leadership that takes place in an interprofessional team is another essential element to effective team functioning. Leadership is best understood in terms of functions performed rather than in terms of a specific person or set of personality traits (Sampson and Marthas, 1981). Leadership functions are actions and behaviors that any team member may carry out, but the leader generally takes responsibility for them. The functions of the leader often include the following (Lippitt, 1961, p. 200):

- ■ helping the team decide on its purpose and goals
- ■ helping the team focus on its own process of working together so that it may become more effective rather than becoming trapped in faulty methods of problem-solving and decision-making

- helping the team to become aware of its own resources and how best to use them
- helping the team to evaluate its progress and development
- helping the team to be open to new and different ideas without becoming immobilized by conflict
- helping the team to learn from its failures and frustrations as well as from its successes

Leadership functions also play a key part in facilitating the interprofessional team through its various developmental stages in order to achieve the desired outcome—namely a higher level of thinking about complex situations that require interprofessional collaboration, planning, and intervention. The leader, then, must attend to a balance of both task and maintenance functions to achieve the intended goals of the interprofessional team.

■ *Decision-Making*

In interprofessional teamwork, decision-making is based on the assumption that the wisdom resides in the team (Thelen, 1970; Kane, 1976). Decision-making is the method or methods for examining and evaluating which alternatives to problem-solving are the most likely and feasible for arriving at a solution. Decision-making entails careful examination of the full range of alternatives, weighing the pluses and minuses of each, and searching for and collecting new information for use in evaluating alternatives (Golin and Ducanis, 1981). Arising whenever a situation exists in an interprofessional team that demands agreement by all team members before the team can move ahead, decision-making is one step in the problem-solving process.

Two key features in decision-making are choice and alternatives. If individual team members are not in a position to choose, or if only one course of action is available, there is no decision to be made (Golin and Ducanis, 1981). Teams must reach decisions about goals, strategies, delegation of tasks, and evaluation of outcomes. Dysfunctional decision-making occurs when not everyone participates, not everyone understands, or both.

Decision-making is a skill that can be learned and improved with practice. Kane (1976), quoting Rubin, suggests a set of guidelines for a team decision-making process (p. 325). In order to decide how decisions are to be made or what form is appropriate, a team must determine who has the necessary information to help make a decision, who must be consulted before a decision is reached, and who will be informed after the fact.

Methods of agreeing about which alternative is the best solution have been discussed by Schein (1972) and Brill (1976), among many others.[3] Decision-making methods include decisions made by authority, by majority, by minority, by default, by consensus, and by consent (Janis and Mann, 1977). Seven criteria

---

[3] See also Horwitz (1970) and Rubin and Beckhard (1972) references to "forms" of decision-making.

for evaluating the procedure used in selecting a course of action are discussed by Golin and Ducanis (1981) and include the following: canvass a wide range of alternatives; survey objectives to be fulfilled and the values implicated by the choice; weigh (or map) risks and consequences; search for information relevant to further evaluation of alternatives; assimilate and take account of new information; reexamine consequences; and make provisions for implementing or executing the plan.

■ Conflict Resolution

Conflict and cooperation are conceptualized as part of the same phenomenon. In interprofessional teamwork, conflict is considered essential and, when constructively used, is one of the most productive forms of collaboration (Kane, 1976; Brill, 1976). Conflict will occur as individuals identify their interests and incompatible goals arise, and its resolution is possible when efforts are made to legitimize and accommodate the differences. The manner in which the team resolves conflicts and reaches decisions will at once contribute to and be a measure of its effectiveness.

Conflict occurs in teams at certain general "levels" (Brill, 1976) or in certain "areas" (Golin and Ducanis, 1981), namely: (a) when members have different and incompatible goals and different ideas on how to operationalize those goals; (b) when members perceive threats to their identities or rights; and (c) in allocation of goals, rewards, and resources. For Brieland, Briggs, and Leuenberger, on the other hand, conflict within a team originates from "three major sources: the internal needs of the team, that is, the personal and collective needs of the individual members; the demands of the external environment, consisting of the organization and the needs of the consumer; and the quality of leadership" (1973, p. 27). Rubin et al. (1975), Germain (1984), and Sands et al. (1990) have presented and discussed the typical approaches or styles employed for the management of conflict in interprofessional teams including avoidance, or smoothing it over; exertion of power, or forcing a solution through domination; compromising, or bargaining; withdrawing from the situation; confrontation, also referred to as consensus or integration, or the open discussion of conflict, analysis of causes, and problem-solving.

The following strategies to prevent, reduce, or deal with conflict in interprofessional teams are consistently found and repeated in the literature:

1. A built-in process to review decisions, including review and definition of goals, the direction of the team, and priorities.
2. The opportunity for each member to develop working knowledge about the others' fields.
3. Autonomy for the professionals on the team to conduct their research.
4. The opportunity for role clarification, including the discussion of topics such as knowledge base, professional stereotypes, specialization, auton-

omy, identification of competencies and responsibilities, and interpretation of the codes of ethics.

5. An examination of overlapping roles and renegotiation of role assignments.
6. A recognition of professional hierarchies and discussion of their impact on team functioning (status and delegation of authority issues are a part of this activity).
7. Improvement of the interprofessional skills of team members—processes for handling conflict can be taught and learned.

Brill has elaborated how conflict may be used constructively in interprofessional teams: by accepting that conflict is normal; by creating a climate in which there is freedom to be different, to disagree, and to express feelings about these differences; by defining the reality of the conflict, its sources, its boundaries, and its possible solutions; by delineating the areas of trust and agreement that do exist; and by considering the various alternatives that might lead to a solution (1976).

In order to manage conflict successfully, members have to move beyond rhetoric and share and explore their own personal objectives in order to manage conflict so that tasks can proceed. As a general rule, the "practical model for dealing with conflict is one which takes the dimensions of personal goals and the concerns for relationships into account" (Hooyman, 1984).

ASSETS AND LIMITATIONS OF THE INTERPROFESSIONAL TEAM

The most common criticism of interprofessional teamwork is the amount of time required to get the job done. The work of the interprofessional team must consciously integrate the processes embedded in the interprofessional team. Engagement of the interprofessional team in honest, reflective appraisal of the complementary nature of the task and maintenance functions inherent in team process will strengthen both the meaning and the success of the interprofessional team.

Who benefits from the interprofessional team? The recipient of services, the team member, the profession, and society as a whole all benefit from interprofessional collaboration. The team member finds support, affirmation, and affiliation for personal and professional growth and development. The profession benefits through strengthening and clarifying professional boundaries; the interprofessional collaboration will be seen as a necessary part of the practice of professionals in a complex society. The individual recipient and society benefit from the elimination of duplication and fragmentation of services. The authors believe that interprofessional interventions will result in a higher quality of service.

INTEGRATION OF TASK AND MAINTENANCE FUNCTIONS FOR EFFECTIVE INTERPROFESSIONAL INTERACTION

Throughout the life of the interprofessional group, each member of the group and the group as a whole have a responsibility for and must participate in maintaining the dynamic balance between task and maintenance functions. Effective group process requires both the analysis and synthesis of the sub-processes and the "reflective appraisal" of completed actions of the interprofessional groups. These processes, as pointed out by Billups (1987), occur simultaneously rather than sequentially in the life of the group. Although these processes occur naturally as part of group life, the delicate balance required will not likewise occur naturally; it must be worked on consciously by the group.

For effective group functioning it is therefore essential that some kind of structure be built into the group to ensure that reflective appraisal does in fact occur. Suggested structures include the following:

1. Agenda setting: In each group meeting allot a portion of the meeting for reflective appraisal by the group.
2. Responsibility for maintenance roles: Appoint or select a team member to assume leadership of the group for reflective appraisal of group actions. Some group process experts have suggested that interdisciplinary groups have coleaders—one leader for task functions, one leader for maintenance functions.
3. Formative evaluation: Build into the group structure a plan for ongoing evaluation of the group's progress.
4. Summative evaluation: Conduct evaluation upon completion of the group task.

Three criteria to judge the effectiveness of group functioning in interprofessional groups must be included: adherence to group structure by both individuals and the group as a whole; the quality of the completed task; and the quality of reflective appraisal of group maintenance functions.

An evaluation of group effectiveness is complete only when all three criteria are applied to the interprofessional group. The complexity of interactive processes in group life will become more apparent if all three criteria are accounted for by the group. Recognition and identification of the multiple interactions that occur simultaneously in group life will clarify the strengths and weaknesses of interprofessional group work.

REFERENCES AND RELATED READINGS

Anthony, E. J. (1971). The history of group psychotherapy. In Kaplan, H. I., and Sadock, B. J. (Eds.), *Comprehensive psychotherapy*. Baltimore: Williams and Wilkens.

Barker, L. (1922). Specialists and general practitioners in relation to teamwork in medical practice. *Journal of the American Medical Association, 78,* 773–779.

Billups, J. O. (1987). Interprofessional team process. *Theory Into Practice, 26*(2), 146–152.

Brieland, D., Briggs, T., and Leuenberger, P. (1973). *The team model of social work practice.* New York: Syracuse University Press.

Brill, N. (1976). *Teamwork: Working together in the human services.* Philadelphia: Lippincott.

Davidson, K. (1990). Role blurring and the hospital social worker's search for a clear domain. *Health and Social Work, 15*(3), 228–234.

Dewey, J. (1904). *The educational situation.* Chicago: University of Chicago Press.

Dewey, J. (1916). *Democracy and education.* New York: MacMillan.

Dewey, J. (1966). *Democracy and education: An introduction to the philosophy of education.* New York: The Free Press.

Dilorio, C., Lehr, S., and Keen, P. (1989). Group dynamics within long-term continuing education programs. *Journal of Continuing Education in Nursing, 20*(1), 24–29.

Ephross, P., and Vasil, T. (1988). *Groups that work: Structure and process.* New York: Columbia University Press.

Farley, M. (1989). The nurse executive and interdisciplinary team building. *Nursing Administration Quarterly, 13*(2), 24–30.

Garner, H. (1988). *Helping others through teamwork.* Washington, DC: Welfare League of America.

Germain, C. B. (1984). *Social work practice in health care: An ecological perspective.* New York: The Free Press.

Golin, A., and Ducanis, A. (1981). *The interdisciplinary team.* Rockville, MD: Aspen.

Harbaugh, G. L., Casto, R. M., and Burgess-Ellison, J. A. (1987). Becoming professional: How interprofessional training helps. *Theory into practice, 26*(2), 141–145.

Holfstein, S. (1964). The nature of process: Its implications for social work. *Journal of Social Work Processes, 14.*

Hooyman, G. (1984). Team building in human services. In Compton, B., and Galaway, B. (Eds.), *Social Work Processes.* Chicago: Dorsey Press.

Horwitz, J. (1970). *Team Practice and the specialist: An introduction to interdisciplinary teamwork.* Chicago: Charles C Thomas.

Jamie, S. (1989). *Teamwork.* New York: Bantam Books.

Janis, I. L., and Mann, L. (1977). *Decision making.* New York: Free Press.

Janosik, E. H., and Phipps, L. B. (1982). *Life cycle group work in nursing.* Monterey, CA: Wadsworth Health Sciences Division.

Johnson, D. W., and Johnson, F. P. (1975). *Joining together: Group theory and group skills.* Englewood Cliffs, NJ: Prentice-Hall.

Kane, R. (1975a). The interprofessional team as a small group. *Social Work in Health Care, 1,* 19–30.

————. (1975b). *Interprofessional teamwork*. New York: Syracuse University School of Social Work.

————. (March 1, 1976). *A profile of interprofessional teamwork practice*. Paper presented at the Annual Program Meeting, Council on Social Work Education, Philadelphia.

Klein, J. (1990). *Interdisciplinarity: History, theory, and practice*. Detroit: Wayne State University.

Larson, C., and LaFasto, F. (1989). *Teamwork: What must go right, what can go wrong*. Beverly Hills: Sage.

Leca, P., and McNeil, J. (1985). *Interdisciplinary team practice: Issues and trends*. New York: Praeger.

Lewin, K. (1951). *Field theory in social sciences: Selected theoretical papers*. New York: Harper & Row.

Lieberman, M. A., Yalom, I. K., and Miles, M. B. (1973). *Encounter groups: First facts*. New York: Basic Books.

Lippitt, G. (1961). How to get results from a group. In Bradford, L. P. (Ed.). *Group Development*. Washington, DC: National Training Laboratories, National Education Association.

Lister, L. (February 1982). Role training for interdisciplinary health teams. *Health and Social Work, 7*(1), 19–25.

Loomis, M. (1979). *Group processes for nurses*. St. Louis: C.V. Mosby.

Lowe, J., and Herramen, M. (1978). Understanding teamwork: Another look at the concepts. *Social Work in Health Care, 3*(3), 323–330.

————. (1981). Understanding teamwork: Another look at the concepts, *Social Work in Health Care, 7*(2), 1–11.

Marram, G. (1978). *The group approach in nursing practice*. St. Louis: C.V. Mosby.

Moreno, J. (1951). *Sociometry: Experimental method and the science of society*. New York: Beacon House.

Napier, R., and Gershenfeld, M. (1993). *Groups: Theory and experience*. Boston: Houghton Mifflin.

New, P. K.-M. (1968). An analysis of the concept of teamwork. *Community Mental Health Journal, 4*(4), 326–333.

Odhner, F. (1970). Group dynamics of the interdisciplinary team. *American Journal of Occupational Therapy, 24*(7), 484–487.

Pepper, B. (1984). The primary group at work. In Germain, C. (Ed.), *Social work practice in health care: An ecological perspective*. New York: The Free Press.

Phipps, L. B. (1982). *Group work: History and overview in life cycle group work in nursing*. Monterey, CA: Wadsworth Health Sciences Division.

Rubin, I., and Beckhard, R. (1972). Factors influencing the effectiveness of health teams. *Milbank Memorial Fund Quarterly, 50*, 317–335.

Rubin, I., Fry, R., and Plovnick, M. (1975). *Improving the coordination of care: A program for health team development*. Cambridge, MA: Ballinger.

Sampson, E. E., and Marthas, M. S. (1981). *Group Process for the Health Professions*. New York: Wiley.

Sands, R., Stafford, J., and McClelland, M. (1990). I beg to differ: Conflict in the interdisciplinary team. *Social Work in Health Care, 14*(3), 55–72.

Schein, E. (1972). *Professional education: Some new directions.* New York: McGraw-Hill.

Schmitt, M. Working together in health care teams. In Janosik, E., and Phipps, E. (Eds.), *Life cycle group work in nursing.* Monterey, CA: Wadsworth Health Sciences Division.

Sieg, W. (1990). *Acting and reflecting: The interdisciplinary turn in philosophy.* Boston: Kluwer Academic.

Steinberg, D. (1989). *Interprofessional consultation: Innovation and imagination in working relationships.* Chicago: Year Book Medical.

Thelen, H. (1970). *Dynamics of groups at work.* Chicago: University of Chicago Press.

Walsh, C. (1991). Collaborative practice: A coordinated approach to patient care. *Orthopaedic Nursing, 10*(5), 52–60.

Yalom, I. D. (1975). *The theory and practice of group psychotherapy.* New York: Basic Books.

PART 3

A Way of Responding

The Methodology of Interprofessional Care and Collaborative Practice

CHAPTER 6

Interprofessional Collaboration
Factors That Affect Form, Function, and Structure

Edward T. Bope, M.D.
Timothy S. Jost, J.D.

Collaboration among professionals takes many different forms. The task to be accomplished; the professional skills available; and geographic, legal, and financial constraints will greatly influence the form. The more common forms of collaborative practice are conferring, cooperating, consulting, multiple entry, and teamwork (Germain, 1984, pp. 204–209). These forms will be discussed along with the factors that may dictate their structures.

Conferring, the simplest form of interprofessional collaboration, is the informal sharing of observations. Conferring is common when professionals trust and respect one another. A physician, nurse, or social worker might confer with a nurse from a home health agency to check whether plans are set for the discharge of an elderly patient. A teacher might confer with a physician about a child with a learning disability who is the pupil of one and the patient of the other. Likewise, a lawyer might confer with a partner regarding a particular case or point of law.

Professionals often cooperate by sharing ideas and knowledge. Cooperation among professionals is less formally structured than the other types of collaborative care. For example, a minister who confers with a physician regarding a troubled parishioner might agree to cooperate in bringing the person to treatment.

Consulting is a form of collaboration in which one professional seeks from another an opinion, often in writing. As when professionals confer, a professional may or may not follow the advice so solicited. However, the professional who sought the consultation will seriously consider the information received. An example is a social worker at a shelter for abused women and children who consults the agency lawyer for an opinion about the advisability of seeking a restraining order.

The multiple entry form involves professionals conferring, cooperating, and consulting on a single case over a period of time, some entering late and others leaving early as the client's needs dictate. For example, a teacher of a child having difficulty learning might ask the child's parents to have their child seen by a physician to rule out minimal brain dysfunction (referring); the physician might then telephone the teacher for an opinion (conferring); together they may decide to ask the school psychologist to do psychological testing (cooperating to consult); and, finally, after that report, they may proceed to a trial of medication under observation while in the class setting (cooperating). The student may have a different teacher each year, with each teacher entering and leaving the child's treatment team (for more on longitudinal care, see Chapter 7).

The last form of collaboration we consider is teamwork. The classic team is rooted historically in the health care industry. The term *team* has both a generic and a specific meaning. T. O. Carlton, in *Clinical Social Work and Health* (1984, pp. 127–129), points out that most people employed at health care facilities feel in a general way that they are part of a team. This abstract and general meaning is broad enough to include virtually any form of collaboration. More narrowly, a team is also a specific group of people who work in a structured manner to deliver human services. Interprofessional teams as thus specifically defined will be the primary focus of this chapter, since teams of this nature have been the focus of our work together and have proved one of the most fruitful forms of interprofessional collaboration. This emphasis is intended to demonstrate the flexibility and adaptability of formal, as well as informal, modes of interprofessional collaboration.

INTERPROFESSIONAL TEAMS

Teams are defined groups of professionals that consult, confer, and cooperate formally and deliberately over a considerable period of time. Teams vary in composition. A typical health-care team might include a nurse, physician, social worker, and various therapists and technical professionals. Increasingly, teams commonly also include a chaplain or pharmacist. Rosalie Kane (1983, p. 50) studied 229 teams that had been the subjects of journal articles and found that professionals appeared on these teams with the following frequency:

Profession	No. of Teams	%
Social Worker	189	82.5
Nurse	150	65.5
Physician	126	59.4
Psychologist	112	48.9
Psychiatrist	94	41.0
Occupational therapist, physical therapist, speech therapist	65	28.4
Teacher	60	26.1
Dietitian	35	15
Vocational counselor	34	14.8
Administrator	22	9.6
Recreationist	18	8.0
Clergy	15	6.6
Researcher	8	3.5
Pharmacist	6	2.6
Lawyer	4	1.7
Engineer	4	1.7
Health educator	4	1.7

The classic health care team has a broadly defined goal of delivering interdisciplinary client care. The physician usually remains responsible for care given by a health care team in that the physician is legally liable for that care, but liability need not dictate leadership of the team. Though nonphysician team members offer advice and render treatment within their professional expertise, the generally held expectation that the physician will lead a health care team often bears itself out in reality, at least initially. Often, however, on a case-by-case basis, a professional with particular interest or expertise in a particular case assumes the leadership. This more functional assignment of leadership often makes sense and should be encouraged.

Kane studied leadership in 138 teams and found that physicians led 65.2 percent of the teams; social workers, 9.4 percent of the teams; educators, 8 percent; managers or administrators, 7.2 percent; nurses, 2.2 percent; and psychologists, 1.4 percent (1983, p. 52). Physicians may be prevalent as leaders on the teams Kane studied, though, because Kane's research was based on literature from the late 1960s and early 1970s when interprofessional teams were uncommon outside of health care settings. In settings outside health care, such as educational or social service institutions, team membership and leadership may look quite different.

Team decisions are often made by consensus, with deference to the opinions of professionals with the most relevant professional experience. For example, most team members may agree that an elderly patient would be happier without a catheter, but the team nurse informs them that the patient's incontinence would in a short period of time macerate fragile skin and lead to further debility. The collegial team would defer, recommending that removing the catheter be reconsidered by a specified date. Often the contribution or the expertise of several members of the interprofessional team will be relevant to a client's problem. The outcome of a team discussion, examining the situation from several perspectives, will yield a decision that is more suitable, comprehensive, and creative than the decision any one member of the team might have reached alone.

The classic team meets for about 60 to 90 minutes to discuss cases, with the frequency of meetings and the number of cases discussed at meetings varying with caseload. Keeping the team meeting so short means that some of the professionals must spend time outside the team meeting studying the case or conferring with colleagues.

ALTERNATIVE FUNCTIONS AND STRUCTURE OF TEAMS

Teams may vary from the aforementioned classic form in purpose, composition, and structure. Though the health care team is probably still the most common, teams frequently appear in other settings. Educational teams, formed to teach a specific curriculum to a specific group of people, are quite common. Examples would be teams to educate individual clients on health issues like prenatal, neonatal, and diabetes self-care; or teams to educate the community about problems such as teen pregnancy and substance abuse. The public school teacher, administrator, school nurse, and school psychologist can function as a team with education and child welfare as the team purpose. Teams may also form around particular problems or issues in education, such as difficult students and truancy. The educational team has taken on particular prominence in dealing with disabled children, for whom the law now requires the development of an individual education plan with interprofessional input.

Research teams study social or medical problems, for instance the effect of a new drug on a population or the incidence of hepatitis, child abuse, or school phobia in a selected area. An evaluation team might monitor blood usage or handle quality assurance in a hospital. Teams are also commonly used to evaluate clients. For example, a team composed of lawyers, social workers, chaplains, school officials, and law enforcement officers might evaluate juvenile offenders to determine an appropriate rehabilitation program. Similarly, teams might evaluate ex-offenders, the mentally disabled, competing child custody arrangements, or patients being discharged from hospitals.

Medical ethics committees are usually interprofessional and deal with the difficult ethical decisions that arise in the modern medical institution. Boards of tax-exempt human services institutions frequently include people of varying professional backgrounds and function, and thus resemble interprofessional teams. Community problems are addressed by advisory boards or policy-making teams, cooperating to serve as consultants to elected leaders. Professional and interprofessional groups have also worked on national and international problems such as nuclear weapons control. A problem like AIDS presents an ideal opportunity for interprofessional collaboration at the institutional, local, state, federal, and international levels, in order to address the myriad, complex issues AIDS presents in the legal, medical, nursing, educational, sociological, psychological, and theological disciplines.

Teams may vary widely in structure. The multiple entry model of collaboration mentioned earlier is discussed further in Chapter 7. This model represents the most common team structure. Another common structure is a small, stable, basic team that frequently consults or confers with other professionals. For example, a team could consist of three or four permanent members but pull in other professionals as needed. This model offers stability and economy while also offering access to a wide variety of skills. A third model for dealing with complex problems of research, administration, or social policy formation is the two-tier team, in which groups meet independently to address different aspects of the problem, then send representatives to meet together, report output, and synthesize results. Although the appropriate structure for collaboration is frequently suggested by the purpose the collaboration is to serve, several structures are often possible, and structure may ultimately be determined by other considerations, such as administrative or fiscal constraints.

FACTORS AFFECTING FORMS OF COLLABORATION

Licensing, liability, and reimbursement issues may affect whether or not professionals form teams and the nature of the teams they form. In an ideal world, external constraints would not distract from service to a client. In the real world, such issues must be considered in determining team form, though every effort should be made to keep them from compromising client services.

Concerns about licensing and scope of practice may influence team composition and structure. Statutes in many states define the practice of medicine in terms of medical diagnosis and treatment and forbid the practice of medicine by any but physicians. In such jurisdictions, a team engaged in medical diagnosis and treatment must include a physician. As mentioned before, the physician would not necessarily need to be the leader of the team but would need to be prepared to take responsibility for its decisions.

Liability concerns may also influence the nature of the team. When team members are jointly caring for a client, each will be individually responsible for his or her own negligence if it results in injury to a client. If a team jointly makes a negligent decision that harms a client, all team members who participated in the decision may be liable to the client (Louisell and Williams, 1988, pp. 16-20–16-21). A team member who is not individually negligent may be liable for the negligence of other team members who were his or her employees acting within the scope of their employment (Louisell and Williams, 1988, p. 16-6). Further, if a professional who initially has contact with a client negligently refers the client to another team member (for example, referring the client to an incompetent professional whom the referring professional knows or should know to be such), the referring professional could be liable for injury caused by the other team member (Louisell and Williams, 1988, p. 16-18). Similarly, a professional who negligently chooses a consultant may be liable for injuries caused by the client's following the consultant's advice.

Once a team undertakes serving a client, it cannot terminate its service until the client's problem is solved, it is discharged by the client, or it withdraws from treatment by making a proper and timely referral (Louisell and Williams, 1988, pp. 8-113–8-119). Any one member can probably withdraw as long as the remaining team members can adequately serve the client. A consultant called in by a team to consult on a particular problem owes no ongoing obligation to the client once the consultant has provided the particular advice sought. A consultant will also not be held liable for the negligence of the team not attributable to the consultant's advice.

In order to serve clients effectively, and because team members are exposed to negligence through so many and varied routes, all team members must take seriously not only their own responsibility, but also the performance of other team members. Though this concern does not necessarily dictate team structure and makeup, team participants should assure themselves that the team has adequate resources to deal with the problem at hand and that each team member is competent. Regardless of the form of leadership and structure a team chooses, some member or members must take responsibility for overseeing team decision-making and implementation. Practically speaking, team members with the most assets or insurance are the most likely targets of malpractice litigation. Thus, these members have added incentives to assure the quality of team performance in both decision-making and implementation.

Institutions may be held liable for injuries caused by the negligent acts of their employees, including teams (Miller, 1990, pp. 192–194). Institutions may even be held liable for the acts of nonemployees who participate in a team if the client justifiably believes the team member to be an employee of the institution (Miller, 1990, pp. 194–195). Finally, institutions may also be held liable for the acts of teams that include both employees and nonemployees, if the employees are jointly liable for the injuries caused by the negligence of the team. Since institutions that deliver human services are generally well insured and often have substantial assets, they are natural targets for malpractice litigation. It is thus essential that they adequately monitor and supervise work that takes place within them, including team service delivery.

Reimbursement issues may also affect team form. If survival of the team depends on third-party payment—from Medicare, Medicaid, Blue Cross, Blue Shield, or commercial insurance—services from team members must be billed by someone licensed to provide the services (usually a physician or nurse) who has earned payment by providing these services. This responsibility may affect team leadership. Consultations needed by the group or ordered for the client must be paid for unless charity has been solicited. In every case the client should be made aware of projected costs of care and consultation.

RAMIFICATIONS OF FORMS OF COLLABORATION

Collaborating professionals must record team functioning and be sensitive to issues of confidentiality and informed consent. Different types of teams may approach these issues in different ways.

Teams depend on communication to hold themselves together and to serve their clients. Good communication is important and has been discussed in Chapter 5. One form of communication is record-keeping. The extent and nature of team records will naturally vary with team purpose and composition. Policy-making, planning, teaching, and administration teams might keep their records in the form of minutes. Health care and consultation team records may be found in the individual medical or social service records of the team's particular clients. Research teams will keep records that reflect the form of research they are conducting. Teams that keep records on individual clients may also want to keep records on the ongoing activity of the team itself.

Though record-keeping is essential in any human service endeavor for treatment, reimbursement, and liability purposes, it is particularly important for human services teams. Records allow team members who have been absent from any particular meeting to conveniently find out what transpired. Team members, particularly new ones, can use records to research a particular client's history. Records facilitate the work of consultants, who can review the previous developments in particular cases. Multiple entry teams find records particularly important, since members rely on the record to determine what else is being done or has been done for a particular client. Indeed, records are often the glue that holds multiple entry teams together, permitting interprofessional collaboration.

Keeping client confidences is the ethical obligation of every human services professional. Assurance of confidentiality is essential if clients are to trust professionals enough to disclose their thoughts, feelings, discomforts, and problems. Full client disclosure is, in turn, essential if professionals are to make informed decisions about their clients. Disclosure of client confidences is not only unethical but violates legal obligations as well. It is therefore important for each team to have a set policy and standard. Professionals who disclose client confidences can be held liable for damages under a variety of legal theories (Roach, Chernoff, and Esley, 1985, pp. 141–157). Confidentiality is important in research as well as in treatment and is protected by federal regulations concerning research on human subjects (45 C.F.R. 46.111[a][7]).

When clients are being cared for within health care or other human services institutions, institutional policies will generally permit access to the records for treatment purposes by professionals practicing in the institution (Roach, Chernoff, and Esley, 1985, pp. 90–91). Thus, as long as a team is wholly composed of professionals employed by or with treatment privileges at an institution, the team nature of treatment will not pose confidentiality problems. To some extent, confidentiality can also be protected in some settings, such as research and teaching, by masking client identity through changing or concealing identifying information. When team members or consultants are brought in from outside the institution, however, it would be wise to obtain client consent for any disclosures. Moreover, when teams are composed of individual professionals with no institutional relationship, client consent to the membership of the team and to disclosures should be obtained.

Informed client consent is also important for team activities directed toward implementing the interprofessional plan. Human services professionals are by now universally familiar with the doctrine of informed consent, which mandates that professionals obtain consent from their clients prior to treatment and that the client receive, prior to giving his or her consent, information concerning the nature of the treatment, its purpose, its risks, and possible alternatives (Miller, 1990, pp. 243–245). When an interprofessional team is engaged in treatment, the client should also be informed of the composition of the team and of the respective roles of its members. Team involvement may complicate the task of informing the client, since team treatment plans may be quite complex. On the other hand, interprofessional teamwork may facilitate the task of obtaining informed consent, since the team may be able to identify members with superior communications skills to assist in this process. Moreover, teams may be more sensitive toward the needs of the whole client and may encourage client involvement in formulating the treatment plan, thus ensuring fuller client understanding of and cooperation with the treatment process—the goal of the informed consent doctrine.

CONCLUSION

Interprofessional collaboration in general, along with teamwork in particular, varies considerably in form and function. Often a generic description of teams poorly describes a particular team. Though a team's form is usually secondary to its task, success at its task will often depend on the suitability of its form. This chapter has considered circumstances that might determine or alter the form of a team. Though this discussion deserves reflection, in reality the mature team with mature professionals will deal with problems of form and function early on, then alter and adapt its determinations as needed to accomplish its tasks. In reality, each member will be obligated to share team responsibility and privileged to share its rewards.

REFERENCES AND RELATED READINGS

Carlton, T. O. (1984). *Clinical social work in health settings.* New York: Springer.

Fagin, C. M. (May 1992). Collaboration between nurses and physicians: No longer a choice. *Academic Medicine, 67*(5), 295–303.

Friend, M., and Cooke, L. (1992). *Interactions: Collaboration skills for school professionals.* White Plains, NY: Longman.

Germain, C. B. (1984). *Social work practice in health care: An ecological perspective.* New York: The Free Press.

Ilott, J. E. D., and Ilott, H. G. (1992). *Diverse models of collaboration in teacher education.* Unpublished paper.

Kane, R. A. (1983). *Interprofessional teamwork.* New York: Syracuse University School of Social Work.

Louisell, D. W., and Williams, H. (1988). *Medical malpractice* (Vol. 1). New York: Matthew Bender.

Lowther, N. B. (1991). A model of interdisciplinary care delivery. In J. R. Snyder (Ed.), *Interdisciplinary health care teams: Proceedings of the thirteenth annual conference* (pp. 98–104). Indianapolis: Indiana University.

McConnell, T. A., et al. (February 1992). Implementation of a team concept of patient care. *Journal of Dental Education, 56*(2), 140–143.

Melaville, A. I., and Blank, M. J. (1993). *Together we can: A guide for crafting a profamily system of education and human services.* Washington, DC: U.S. Department of Education and U.S. Department of Health and Human Services.

Miller, R. D. (1990). *Problems in hospital law* (6th ed.). Germantown, MD: Aspen Systems.

Roach, W. H., Chernoff, S. N., and Esley, C. L. (1985). *Medical records and the law.* Germantown, MD: Aspen Systems.

Swezey, R. W., et al. (February 1992). Ensuring teamwork: A checklist for use in designing team training programs. *Performance and Instruction, 31*(2), 33–37.

CHAPTER 7

Prospective Management and Longitudinal Care
The Dynamic Changing Nature of Team Activity

Daniel B. Lee, D.S.W.
P. Tennyson Williams, M.D.

This chapter focuses on preventive opportunities for interprofessional care. We will discuss the dynamic nature of changes in individuals' situations, creating the need for change in the roles of interprofessional team members. The discussion will give attention to the process of longitudinal care and illustrate the longitudinal development of individual problems. The implications for changing team relationships resulting from dynamic changes occurring to clients over time will also be considered. We will offer the identification of risk factors as one approach to the development of strategies to prevent or minimize later dysfunctional events.

ASSUMPTIONS

The chapter is organized around five assumptions formulated on the basis of both theoretical and empirical considerations. These assumptions are as follows:

1. Most problems can be prevented, delayed or ameliorated when detected early and managed appropriately.
2. Certain precursors or risk factors increase the probability that specific problems will follow, providing rationale for strategies of early intervention.
3. Different stages of problem development call for different strategies of intervention.
4. These different stages necessitate changing team structure and individual provider roles for effective interprofessional operation.
5. Overcoming the barriers to effective communication between and among interprofessional care team members is central to the process of longitudinal care.

These assumptions are congruent with common assumptions about interprofessional practice:

1. The interprofessional approach produces effective resolution of multifaceted complex client problems.
2. Effective team operation is based upon mutual recognition and appreciation of the role and resources of each participating interprofessional.
3. The evaluation process assures the client and interprofessional team members of benefit and satisfaction.

■ *Professional Heritage*

Understanding the heritage of each profession is necessary for a proper consideration of these assumptions. Discussion of the medical profession can serve as one model for how such a consideration might proceed.

Physicians come to the table of interprofessional care from a long tradition and experience of *multidisciplinary* care, in which several doctors are involved in caring for a given patient. This background has created a bias that may serve as a barrier to the functioning of the interprofessional team a physician joins. It is useful for other members to understand the roles physicians have become accustomed to assume.

Primary care physicians have recently been trained to coordinate the recommendations of consultants and to integrate the recommendations of allied health professionals and consultants from other professions. The physician must accept a coordinating role, while the other professionals must trust one person's judgment about whether and how to accept and implement recommendations from a variety of sources. These interpersonal relationships are dyadic, with the same referring physician always one member of the dyad.

Most of the literature on team development and management appearing in medical journals refers to multidisciplinary teams of physicians; interdisciplinary team development and management generally refers to health professionals other than physicians. (In other professional literatures this same distinction is not necessarily made.) Consequently, *interdisciplinary* care is not a part of physicians' usual experience, except when referral is into an interdisciplinary situation such as a mental health center, where a health care team will deal with a patient.

However, some referrals ultimately result in high-technology procedures such as open-heart surgery. These referrals require the supporting activities of several allied health and other professionals. Such cases are a part of the medical milieu and do not reflect true interprofessional team function. In these cases, roles are determined by rigid protocols, and activities are always physician-directed.

Robertson (1992) recently described the problems health care teams experience in care of the elderly: "physicians must refer and interact appropriately with other health professionals in addressing the multiple and complex needs of elderly patients." He described five circumstances in which a multidisciplinary team offers advantages over monodisciplinary (medical) care (p. 136):

1. when the perspectives of other health disciplines are vital to a comprehensive understanding of a patient's health or social needs
2. when sharing information is of mutual benefit
3. when decisions regarding future actions (treatment, rehabilitation, facility placement, or community services) must be negotiated rather than prescribed
4. when various medical and social interventions must be coordinated
5. when interaction between patient, caregiver, health care workers, and other professionals is essential

Robertson also differentiated between multidisciplinary and interdisciplinary teams, assigning the latter a greater role of collaboration and negotiating patient management goals in face-to-face meetings. He cautioned that complex patient problems may call for the input of a large number and variety of health professionals and that the team becomes inefficient and loses focus unless a core or nuclear team consisting of a representative of each discipline is designated (for example, one person each from medicine, nursing, rehabilitation therapy, and social work).

Physicians' unique professional heritage clearly influences their relationship to interprofessional teams. Other professionals also have unique heritages that affect their collaborative practice. Team members must be familiar with and give due consideration to the heritage and assumptions of each professional on the team if the team is to effectively fulfill its goals.

We will now discuss the concepts underlying each of the five assumptions presented earlier, concerning the problems that interprofessional teams work on. We will present the clinical application of these assumptions, and look at how the collaborative roles of human service professionals apply to several clinical cases.

■ Assumption One

Most problems can be prevented, delayed, or ameliorated when detected early and managed appropriately. This assumption is based on several concepts of developmental psychology, the Health Belief Model, and the Disease Control Model. An awareness of these concepts assists in developing more effective interventions when health and other professionals comanage client problems. Recognizing whether or not developmental tasks are mastered in proper sequence permits identification of those at high risk of future disorders, some of which may be prevented by appropriate and timely action. The combined skills of different professionals should facilitate the development of an intervention once early clues to problems are identified in high-risk clients. In their simplest form, timely identification and action may mean recognizing early on that consultation with a colleague of another discipline may prevent a future crisis. What we know about human development not only reinforces the importance of early detection, but also informs our understanding of team functioning.

Human development concepts. Developmental theorists, including Erikson, Mahler, Piaget, and Freud, have contributed to our understanding of the sequential unfolding of human growth and development. These theorists have proposed that development occurs gradually over time and that human biological growth and socialization are synchronous processes. Therefore, some events in the life span are antecedents for future events (Vander Zanden, 1981), and their absence increases the probability of later dysfunctional behavior. Lerner et al. (1982) assert that development is represented by the emergence of characteristics at new stages of development that were not present in any previous form prior to their emergence.

The mastery of early developmental tasks is believed to be an important consideration, since failure to resolve those tasks leads to a state of conflict that stands in the way of achieving optimal growth and development (Erikson, 1963). Erikson's stage theory of human development explicates psychosocial tasks and crises throughout the life cycle. For example, bonding precedes trust, which is basic to the development of interpersonal relationships. Perhaps there are counterparts to these stages in the development of interprofessional team member relationships.

Absence or lack of socialization often leads to character disorders such as the undersocialized type of conduct disorder in childhood. If identity crises and role acquisition are not resolved during adolescence, a person may continue to experience an identity struggle throughout adulthood. Likewise, health and other professionals comanaging a client problem must make the effort to clearly identify the role expected of each member of the team.

According to Piaget (1952), it is critical for a person to acquire the cognitive skills necessary to integrate the person's biological, social, and emotional development. Cognitive theorists assert further that belief systems—ways of interpreting, communicating, and problem-solving—are components of the power of cognition and that they can guide human interaction. On the other hand, common misconceptions, irrational ideas, and mistaken beliefs cause and sustain psychological disturbance (Tversky and Kahneman, 1974). For instance, an adolescent girl with anorexia nervosa, an eating disorder, often maintains an irrational belief about her body image that results in delayed psychosexual development. In the case of Jessica (see Chapter 10), misinterpreting the symptomatic problems of her broken leg and her grandson Peter's emotional vulnerability delayed her appropriate problem-solving approach to her husband's chronic alcohol abuse.

The health belief model (HBM). Another key to understanding the beliefs and behavior of patients or clients is the Health Belief Model (HBM). This model evolved from the study of noncompliance of well patients to the interventions of disease prevention programs (Janz and Becker, 1984). It was found that four considerations accounted for most noncompliant behavior:

1. Perceived lack of susceptibility to the disease that the program sought to prevent
2. Perceived lack of severity (risk of death or disability) of the problem in question
3. Perceived lack of personal benefit from the intervention recommended
4. Perceived barriers to the implementation of the recommended interventions

The model also recognizes the patient's attribution underlying those perceptions as it influences cognitive processes. Examples of the application of the HBM include the relationship between patient or client behavior and spouse beliefs, and the correlation between mother's use of wellness physician visits for her baby and her perception of the health status of her baby (Becker et al., 1977). Accurate understanding of the beliefs of patients or clients not only is necessary so that health professionals can individualize appropriate education to enhance compliance, but also permits them to identify health risks at a stage that can lead to prevention or amelioration of the problem at issue.

Careful and frequent monitoring of health beliefs thus becomes an important task for both prospective management and longitudinal care. Health professionals must understand the basis for clients' beliefs and attributions in order to develop care plans that consider barriers to their implementation. For instance, a patient who does not attribute high risk of breast cancer to her situation is unlikely to perform breast self-examination despite adequate education regarding its performance (Janis and Rodin, 1979).

The disease control model. The epidemiological model stresses the role environment plays in influencing both cause and decline of disease. The enactment of public laws mandating testing for phenylkaptonuria (a genetic disease caused by a recessive gene) has virtually eliminated this cause of mental deficiency in children (Berger, 1983). Similarly, public law mandates testing thyroid levels of newborn babies. Undetected thyroid deficiency leads to short stature and mental deficiency. Variation in the density of low-income population, availability of educational materials concerning the impact of diet and drugs on the developing fetus, and adequacy of medical facilities for high-risk newborns explain much of the regional variation in infant mortality and numbers of infants with low birth weight.

Other laws have created major changes in human behavior to the benefit of health care outcomes. The most dramatic of these have been those mandating seat belt use (19 percent compliance in 1983 and 69 percent in 1991) and the installation of smoke detectors (67 percent compliance in 1983 and 88 percent in 1991) (Prevention Index, 1992); also dramatic has been the proliferation of smoke-free environments resulting from municipal regulations and corporate and institutional actions.

When all members of an interprofessional team are aware of the concepts directed to this first assumption, development of common goals for managing individuals' problems becomes easier. The mutual agreement among different professionals necessary to achieve the macro-level results cited here stemmed from professionals sharing these concepts in fulfillment of this assumption.

■ Assumption Two

Precursors of risk factors have been found to increase the probability that certain disorders will follow, providing the rationale for strategies of early intervention that will prevent or modify the disorder. This assumption is based on concepts derived from epidemiological studies and retrospective studies of the natural history of crises. The use of risk factors as the basis for preventive strategies developed from longitudinal studies of populations. For example, the landmark findings of the Framingham study demonstrated that the risk of coronary heart disease can be reduced 90 percent by removing four major risk factors: elevated blood pressure, overweight, elevated cholesterol, and cigarette smoking (Kannel and Sorlie, 1979). Klaus and Kennell (1976) reported that precursors to both child abuse and hyperactivity include a lack of parental bonding at birth, a history of parental neglect and deprivation during the parents' childhood, poor parental self-image, and a culture that relies on corporal punishment. Starfield (1985) has stated that the way to decrease the devastating outcomes of child abuse is through prevention, largely by applying interventions in families identified using the precursors defined by Kempe and Helfer (1980).

Primary prevention as a community health concept involves lowering the rate of new cases of a condition or disorder in a population over a certain period by counteracting harmful circumstances before they have had a chance to produce irreversible changes. Secondary prevention involves reducing the complications from and the progression of an already present disorder. Secondary prevention involves taking a long-term view of the continuing factors that mold the development of a person's general life-style and a short-term view of the recurrent crises associated with sudden changes in patterns of behavior (Caplan, 1964).

For example, the suicide of a grade-school child provides both macro and micro opportunities for the primary prevention of further cases. The school and community may develop programs to provide education regarding the possible precursors so that all may understand potential risk factors and actions they may take (on the macro level). As teachers and parents identify such precursors, individuals may be referred for appropriate interventions (on the micro level). Interprofessional involvement improves the quality of the outcome at both levels.

High-risk conditions subject to preventive interventions may be linked to the life cycle, as set out in Table 7.1.

In the case of Roger (see Chapter 10), an identification of his risk factors might have led to an exploration of his health beliefs (Assumption One), which could have enhanced his compliance with risk reduction and subsequent HIV prevention. Roger is a gay man who had a stable monogamous relationship. The termination of this relationship caused severe stress. His reaction resulted in brief relationships with multiple partners, and ultimately he acquired characteristics of HIV infection. His physician and minister both knew of Roger's sexual orientation before the monogamous relationship had terminated. If they had realized that such a crisis would make inappropriate high-risk behavior probable, they both would have had the opportunity to counsel him about behavior that would reduce exposure to HIV infection.

Crisis theory is anchored in the assumption that an upset in a steady state accompanied by hazardous events requires reestablishment of equilibrium (balance). In a state of crisis, customary problem-solving methods are not adequate and do not lead to the previously achieved state of balance (Rapoport, 1965). Caplan (1964) conceived of four characteristics of crisis development: (1) the initial rise in tension stimulated by stress, (2) the continuous rise in tension associated with ineffective habitual coping mechanisms, (3) the intensified tension calling on the emergency problem-solving mechanisms, and (4) resultant major disorganization.

The solution sought to restore a sense of equilibrium may when implemented result in a return to the prior level of functioning, in a more adequate or higher level of functioning, or in a lower level of functioning (see Figure 7.1). Problem-solving during a state of crisis, according to Rapoport (1965), can be facilitated by the identification and isolation of the factors leading to the disruption of functioning; the caretaker's acceptance of the expression and management of the client's disordered affect, irrational attitudes, or negative responses; and the use of available interpersonal and institutional resources.

Practice implications. The evolution of the natural history of an episode of depression as derived from the history of a specific individual is examined here in order to illustrate the relationship between risk factors and probable level of risk.

A few observations about depression will enhance the appreciation of its relevance to this discussion. Depression occurs in nearly 30 percent of primary care patients and is especially important because of its usually covert presenta-

TABLE 7.1 ■
High-Risk Conditions That Require Preventive Interventions Throughout the Life Cycle (A multiple entry model for interprofessional care)

Life Cycle	High-Risk Conditions	Levels of Prevention (I, II, or III)	Interpro-fessional Multiple Entry
1. Prenatal period (conception to birth)	a. Infertility b. Malnutrition c. Elective termination of pregnancy d. Low birth weight and premature birth e. Birth complications f. Physiological deficits (birth defect) g. Still birth		
2. Infancy (the first 2 years)	a. Infant death b. Adoption* c. Parental deprivation* d. Child maltreatment* e. Lead poisoning		
3. Early childhood (2 to 6)	a. Mental retardation* b. Physically handicapped children* c. Autism d. Fear and anxiety* e. Attention deficit disorder* (hyperactivity) f. Children of divorce and single parenthood*		
4. Later childhood (7 to 12)	a. Learning disability* b. Conduct disorder* c. Emotional disorder* (childhood depression)		
5. Early adolescence (13 to 15)	a. Runaways* b. Juvenile delinquency*		
6. Later adolescence (16 to 18)	a. Substance abuse (alcohol and drugs)* b. Adolescent suicide c. Unwanted pregnancy and teen parentage d. Identity disorder e. School dropouts		

TABLE 7.1 *(continued)* ■

Life Cycle	High-Risk Conditions	Levels of Prevention (I, II, or III)	Interprofessional Multiple Entry
	f. Minority youth and alienation		
	g. Separation and emancipation		
	h. Eating disorder		
7. Young adulthood (19 to 35)	a. Obesity*		
	b. Family planning*		
	c. Marriage (intimacy and mate selection)		
	d. Occupational choice		
	e. Sexual disorders*		
	f. Unemployment*		
	g. Pregnancy*		
	h. Child rearing		
	i. Separation and divorce*		
	j. Domestic violence (spouse abuse)*		
	k. Mental disorders*		
8. Middle adulthood (40 to 60)	a. Menopause		
	b. Job dissatisfaction		
	c. Intergenerational conflict		
	d. Midlife crisis		
	e. Remarriage		
9. Later adulthood (old age, death and dying)	a. Retirement		
	b. Social isolation		
	c. Widowhood		
	d. Dementias		
	e. Death of spouse		
	f. Ill health		
	g. Institutionalization		

*These conditions can occur during the successive developmental periods.

tion with physical symptoms, the most common of which is fatigue (Driscoll et al., 1992; Gerber et al., 1992). In addition, depressive symptoms are associated with more service burden and impairment than clinical conditions or dysthymia. Service burdens include emergency room use; medical consultations; the use of tranquilizers, sleeping pills, and antidepressants; poor self-reported emotional health; days lost from work; and suicide attempts (Johnson et al., 1992). Consequently, primary physicians usually provide mental health services in the context of a concurrent physical condition. Many professionals are trained in

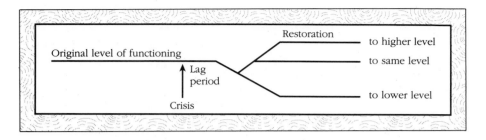

FIGURE 7.1 ■
Crisis development process (Adapted, with permission, from a diagram in *Principles of Family Medicine,* by R. E. Rakel, p. 352. © 1977 by W. B. Saunders.)

counseling and may serve as additional resources for these patients, especially those with milder illnesses (Knesper and Pagnucco, 1987).

The source of reimbursement for medical care has a significant impact on the use of mental health services and thus the ability to implement interdisciplinary care. The probability of initially using such services is roughly the same in the fee-for-service and health maintenance organization (HMO) populations, but the probability of continuing mental health services in the next year is less with an HMO, especially for frequent use as opposed to high number of users (McGuire and Fairbank, 1988). In addition, those receiving prepaid medical care are less likely to have their depression detected or treated than are similar patients receiving fee-for-service care.

Management of depression by primary care physicians has been judged inadequate, though no recommendations for improvement include increasing interdisciplinary care. Instead, preference is given to continuing education for primary physicians (Eisenberg, 1992). The study of outcomes of 'different approaches to care of depression is in its infancy, but so far the use of counseling by allied health and other professionals has not shown improved outcomes. Generalizing the findings of these studies is not useful, given the differences in disease severity, populations of patients, and health-care reimbursement policies. Further study of mental health diagnosis and management must include alternative monodisciplinary, multidisciplinary, and interdisciplinary schemes to determine which is most effective, for which patients, and in which health care system (Brody and Larson, 1992).

A 48-year-old male schoolteacher reported that his recurrent episodes of depression were always preceded by a precipitating event of 2 to 4 weeks' duration. Each episode of depression evolved with the same sequence of events, though the duration of each step in the sequence varied depending on recognition, strength of self-control, and degree of support from significant others.

This sequence is depicted in Figure 7.2, in which the onset (1) was heralded by a feeling of anxiety and of being upset more easily than usual. This feeling was followed by early awakening with difficulty in returning to sleep accompanied by the onset of fatigue (4). It then became significantly more difficult to make decisions as decision-making skills deteriorated (5). This stage

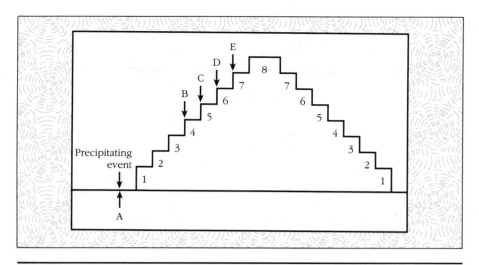

FIGURE 7.2 ■
Natural history of an episode of depression

may be interpreted as a loss of motivation. The teacher then became aware of difficulty in preparing lesson plans and of decreasing ability to maintain his attention on course development and teaching skills (6). He began to experience difficulty in maintaining the organization of his usual administrative tasks (7), and finally home activities and responsibilities became disorganized (8).

The occurrence of a precipitating event (A) presents the first opportunity for anticipating the resulting episode of depression and allows insight into the future provision of an anticipatory guidance intervention prior to a new episode of depression. This knowledge makes it possible for this person to direct his behavior and attempt to maintain a level of motivation that will forestall the full development of future episodes (B). Counseling by a professional would be expected to halt or slow progression at this point. The precipitating event may be seen as a precursor calling for early intervention and leading to the formation of an intervention team. Stages 5 through 8 make a statement of values and priorities. Those of another person might lead to the deterioration of home tasks preceding a change in work performance. Also at this point, other people become involved in both the home and work environment (D). Attitudes and problems created by the changes necessitated in the lives of others might be forestalled if this patient's problems are recognized early on. On the other hand, for those involved to recognize and understand the situation enlarges the supportive network for the client or patient and leads to the establishment of an interprofessional team of mental health professionals and physicians.

The various nodal points in the development of depression in this case demonstrate multiple points of entry for health care providers, as well as illustrate different levels of intervention. The patient, family, and school officials may become involved in identifying a potential problem at the time of the precipitating crisis, leading to behavioral counseling by a single professional or a team of professionals. Before work performance becomes impaired, school officials should become part of the team and participate in developing the criteria necessary to maintain work effectiveness. When medication is necessary (point C), a knowledgeable primary physician or psychiatrist is needed to prescribe and monitor antidepressant medications.

■ Assumption Three

Intervention strategies should be individualized to the stage of problem development.   This assumption is based on concepts derived from the public health model, the strategic intervention model, and the multiple entry model, which all focus on phase-specific intervention approaches to problem solution. The case of S.B. (see Chapter 10) is presented to illustrate different entry points of professionals at various stages of problem development.

Public health model (PHM).   This model proposes three levels of prevention: primary, secondary, and tertiary (Mausner and Kramer, 1985). Primary prevention aims at preventing specific disorders from occurring by promoting positive physical and mental health and eliminating risk factors. Secondary prevention aims at reducing the prevalence and duration of disorders and preventing their complications by early and prompt treatment. Tertiary prevention aims at reducing the severity of and disability associated with a disorder that has already emerged and at delaying the disorder's expected progression. The public health model underlines the dual dimensions of promoting growth and reducing disability. These levels of prevention can occur in personal, social, and environmental contexts. Table 7.2 illustrates individual (micro) and social and environmental (macro) interventions for both growth promotion and disability reduction. Interprofessional collaboration can be organized or instituted around each of these areas or around combined areas of concern. For instance, if the main concern is to reduce family violence, this concern leads inevitably to a macro level of prevention to minimize the adverse impacts of family violence on children, adults, and the community at large. Therefore, the unit of our attention in primary prevention may include not only the individual, couple, or family. It may also extend well beyond a single family unit. Primary prevention may also be directed toward neighborhoods, formal and informal groups and organizations, various identifiable populations, entire communities, and whole societies.

Strategic intervention model (SIM).   This model, which incorporates the concepts of the public health model, was originally developed by LeVine (1962) and was modified by Lee and Williams (1984) for application to the multiple entry model of interprofessional practice in longitudinal care. This model assumes that intervention strategies must be developed and applied to specific stages of client functioning. There are five stages of client functioning:

1. The client's condition requires nonspecific protection and anticipatory guidance.

TABLE 7.2 ■
An Illustrated Matrix of Prevention

	PROMOTION OF GROWTH	REDUCTION OF DISABILITY
INDIVIDUAL LEVEL (MICRO)	Education Protection Promoting competence Assertive training	Crisis intervention Self-screening Stress management Rational-emotive counseling
SOCIAL/ ENVIRONMENT LEVEL (MACRO)	Genetic counseling Family life education Advocacy Social network Consumerism	Ombudsman Reduction of discrimination Environmental protection Accident prevention Reduction of family violence

2. The client's condition requires specific protection.
3. The client's condition requires services for early detection and prompt care.
4. The client's condition requires a strategy to limit disability.
5. The client's condition requires social rehabilitation.

These conditions are on a continuum from a beginning optimal level of social function (eufunction) to a post-deteriorating stage of function (severe dysfunction).

Strategies of intervention are linked to these conditions of client social function and applied to those conditions at various implementation levels of intervention agent(s). There are six levels of implementation:

1. pre-intervention awareness level, with no specific intervention strategy being applied
2. beginning level for anticipation or formulation of intervention
3. assessment for intervention planning and service development
4. provision of need guided by assessment of level of social function
5. intervention directed to host environment to minimize progression
6. conflict resolution of complex dysfunction, always involving other individuals

The progression of disease states is also said to go through six stages, which are parallel to the aforementioned six levels of intervention:

1. risk factor absent, causative factor absent, no signs or symptoms
2. risk present, agent absent, no signs or symptoms
3. risk factor and agent present, no signs or symptoms
4. risk factor and agent present, signs present, no symptoms
5. risk factor and agent present, signs and symptoms present
6. rehabilitation

Figure 7.3 illustrates both stages of client social functioning and levels of intervention as incorporated in the progression of disease in the multiple entry model.

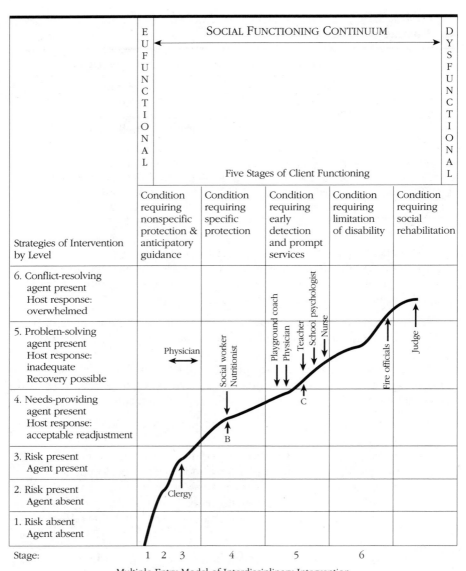

Multiple Entry Model of Interdisciplinary Intervention

FIGURE 7.3 ■
A conceptual model for classification of specific social functioning by state of client functioning and by strategy of intervention (This conceptual model was originally developed by LeVine, 1962, and modified by Lee and Williams, 1984).

Multiple entry model (MEM).   Like the preceding models, the multiple entry model is based on practical considerations of clients' help-seeking behavior, the orientation of health professionals in accommodating their clients' needs and requests, and institutional arrangements for providing services to various population groups over a life-cycle period. No one particular professional seems to carry out a lifelong commitment with all accompanied expertise to meet the varied needs of a client from conception to death. Instead, like passengers on a commuter train, clients seem to get on and off at different stages of their life circumstances requiring the intervention of professionals. MEM is conceptualized in the context of change and life-cycle needs for differential accommodations and has practical implications for interprofessional participation and coordination for longitudinal care of clients or patients.

In the evolution of the natural history of attention deficit disorder, for instance, the members of the interprofessional team may change according to the problem's stage or severity and rate of progression. Therefore the disciplines represented on the team, the role of individual team members, and team leadership undergo dynamic changes over time. The case of S.B. (see Chapter 10) is charted in Figure 7.3, illustrating the need to individualize management according to problem stages.

Application of the models to the case of S.B.   The pregnancy and birth did not provide any clues, as is often the case, to lead the primary care physician to be vigilant for precursors of this newborn boy's future problems. However, at age 4, S.B.'s problems with discipline, failure to learn from previous accidents, and short attention span were sufficiently strong clues to suggest modification of parenting skills in order to decrease the risk that the child would acquire behavioral or learning problems, or both.

These observations might have occurred to the physician or to reception staff had they observed S.B.'s waiting room behavior on the occasion of wellness care visits or illness visits. They might have become obvious to Sunday-school teachers or others in situations involving group activities such as T-ball. A physician, member of the clergy, or coach might have had the opportunity to intervene, offer guidance, or alert parents to potential learning and behavior problems. The physician might have taken the opportunity during the preschool examination to suggest that at their first parent-teacher conference the parents ask the teacher specific questions relating to attention span.

Therefore, the opportunity for team formation and exploration of the case might have appropriately fallen to individuals from several disciplines at various times. Roles would have included identification, recommendation for referral, educational intervention, medication monitoring, and counseling.

Other preschool opportunities might have occurred to emergency room staff caring for accidental injuries or to social workers who might have been asked to investigate the source of recurrent accidents. In addition, an alert parent might have sought relief from one of several resources. Questions about the relationship of diet to hyperactive behavior might have been asked of a nutritionist or home health agent. It would have been appropriate at the time of school entry to request an evaluation by the school psychologist.

S.B. proceeded to have difficulty in the classroom and to engage in behavior outside the classroom that comes to the attention of the local police, judge, and legal representative.

When professionals enter a case from different disciplines, as in the MEM, several tasks become important for maintaining continuity. This significantly complicates the process by requiring tasks that may not have been modeled in professional training. These tasks are called for by the following needs:

1. the need for a data base "depository" that is available for sharing with other professionals as the natural history of the problem unfolds
2. the need for individual professionals to be able to assume different roles at different times in the evolution of patient problems (for example, at times the physician had the opportunity to be the sole provider, to be the team leader in a coordinated effort, and to integrate the care of others by sharing previous reports when not otherwise involved)
3. the need for roles and tasks to be specifically defined when more than one provider is involved, including the identification of others with whom reports are to be shared
4. the need for flexibility in team formation, disbanding, and reformation over time

The problems of maintaining confidentiality while communicating essential information can easily become barriers to optimal interprofessional care and must be addressed continually.

In summary, as illustrated in Figure 7.3, several health professionals had the opportunity to identify early precursors or risk factors. During this time the only interventions were counseling regarding parenting skills, anticipatory guidance regarding natural history, and direction in establishing guidelines for discipline. By the time school performance required evaluation by a school psychologist, prompt services were required. At the stage at which repeated arson episodes were brought to the attention of the judge, social rehabilitation was necessary. Successful intervention at any point had the potential to improve the eventual outcome.

■ Assumption Four

Changing the structure and function of interprofessional operation and individual professional roles is necessitated when a problem progresses to higher stages of behavioral and social dysfunction. Complexity is evident in the course of progressive disorders, whether in the physical or the social domain. Corresponding to problem complexity, intervention strategies often call for a high level of collaboration among professionals when the problem progresses beyond its early stages of development. Interprofessional practice takes many forms, as elaborated in preceding chapters. Issues concerning barriers to interprofessional communication, power dynamics and leadership, ethics, and economy of time and resources are also discussed elsewhere in this book.

Assumption Four underlines the basic concept of systemic approaches to interprofessional care. It emphasizes openness, flexibility, integration, and synthesis among all participating components of interprofessional activity. This assumption applies general systems concepts and ecological perspectives—which stress interrelatedness and synergistic processes—to the changing needs of interprofessional team operation in the context of longitudinal care.

Changing the structure and function of interprofessional behavior, then, becomes a vital process by which professionals can anticipate the changing nature of client problems. As described in Chapter 2, their worldviews guide both clients and professionals in validating the meanings and consequences of problems. If helping professionals take a holistic approach to a problem, interprofessional collaboration becomes a more salient dimension to be explored in the delivery of institutional services. Theoretically, an ecological perspective incorporates values that underlie a concept of development in context. Bronfenbrenner (1979) defines human development as "the process through which the growing person acquires a more extended, differentiated and valid conception of the ecological environment, and becomes motivated and able to engage in activities that reveal the properties of, sustain, or restructure that environment at levels of similar or greater complexity in form and content" (p. 27).

Likewise, interprofessional structural development needs to go through a similar developmental maturation in order to function effectively in response to the changing demands of client ecology. According to Bronfenbrenner, the issue is professionals' capacity to employ effective strategies in providing accurate feedback about the nature of the system (for instance, schoolteachers or primary health care providers in the case of S.B.). These systems exist at successively more remote levels (for instance, the church, the neighborhood community, the legal system, and so on). Professionals enable these systems to continue to function. They reorganize existing systems (for example, a local interprofessional review board for all childhood disability cases) or create new ones of comparable or higher order that are more in accord with the needs of their clients (for instance, a case management system to ensure the continuity, coordination, and quality of longitudinal care).

From a macro-systems perspective, it is important to connect the immediate setting of power (the individual client or professional) with power in the local community and beyond (the interprofessional team). Bronfenbrenner's ecological hypothesis of human development may be likened to the responsive engagement model of interprofessional team development: "The developmental potential of a setting [professionals] is enhanced to the extent that there exist direct and indirect links to power settings [interprofessional team] through which participants in the original setting can influence allocation of resources and the making of decisions that are responsive to the needs of the developing person [client] and the efforts of those who act in his [or her] behalf" (p. 256).

The role played by the natural history of problems, and the well-being of individuals, are the result of individuals' education, experiences, and informal lessons learned from parents and others who touched their lives. Their inner weaknesses can be understood from their failures. Clues to their strengths can be gained from their triumphs. The degree to which they have been tested is judged by the outcomes of their past battles. Their response to future situations can be expected to mirror their past behavior. These tendencies hold for psychosocial behavior as well as for physiological behavior—individuals' fears and joys as well as their headaches and blood pressure.

This, then, is the background necessary for the practice of anticipatory management. Medical technology has wiped out the major common killers and causes of suffering of past years (such as smallpox and polio). Further significant improvement in health care and in the quality of life for U.S. residents depends on a shift from diagnosis and treatment of biologic problems to the modification of destructive human behaviors (like tobacco use, not wearing seat belts, and so on), and improved recognition and management of biopsychologic problems.

■ Assumption Five

Overcoming barriers to effective communication between interprofessional team members is central to the process of longitudinal care. Comanagement in institutional settings where interprofessional teams are trained together has been standardized in respect to the process and participants' roles. This standardization occurs in mental health centers, clinics operating research protocols, transplant operating rooms, and so on. When two or more health professionals provide comanagement outside institutions, however, little standardization of either process or expectations has occurred. Additionally, professionals who have had the opportunity for a long-term association with a client or patient have usually developed with that client or patient a mutual understanding of expectations. Balint (1957) describes this as a "capital investment." He suggests that such professionals should be able to "lend a part of the capital invested" in them by their clients or patients to others called upon to share in managing those clients' or patients' problems. Although Balint's work was with British general practitioners and their consultants, the concept is applicable to the function of interprofessional teams. This aspect of comanagement and team function has received little attention in studies of the consultation process or team function and leadership.

Medical literature on the consultation process reveals priorities different from those prominent in the mental health and allied health literature (Rakel and Williamson, 1984, Ducanis and Golin, 1979). The major problem identified in medical studies is that of communication. Mental health and allied health research cite problems of mutual respect, team leadership, and team formation. Other issues identified in the mental health and allied health literatures include establishment of participant roles and determination of parameters necessary for identifying future nodal points that mandate changes in management strategies. There is also a reasonably good understanding of the consultation and referral process in defining roles and expectations in the acute care setting. By contrast, there is little or no standardization in any literature concerning longitudinal care that involves simultaneous care by more than one professional. In point of fact, the practice settings of many professionals do not provide the human and material resources to support communication with others outside

Date _____

Patient name _____

Team members _____

Problem list _____

_____

Treatment goals _____

_____

Anticipated nodal points

If	Then
_____	_____
_____	_____
_____	_____

Parameters to follow	Intervals	Who
_____	_____	_____
_____	_____	_____
_____	_____	_____

Visit schedule (interval) and role

    Provider _____   Visit interval _____

        Role _____

    Provider _____   Visit interval _____

        Role _____

    Provider _____   Visit interval _____

        Role _____

FORM 1 ■
Shared care worksheet

the immediate office or institution. Therefore, resulting communication problems should not come as a great surprise, especially when ever-present time factors are also considered.

The following plan was developed to enhance decision-making and to facilitate communication in longitudinal care situations. Implementing the plan depends on the use of two instruments: a planning worksheet to direct problem identification and role assignment, and a flow chart for summarizing data.

The planning worksheet (Form 1) is used to define the goals of management and establish the roles of the providers involved. Goals are to be described in terms of (1) changes the intervention is expected to create, (2) "next events"

1° Dx _____   Name _____

Co-Morbidity _____

Date									
BP									
Weight									
Pulse									
Respiration									
Temp									

Summary of problem and status _____

_____

_____

_____

_____

Response desired   Yes   No   (circle) _____

FORM 2 ■
Monitoring flow chart

(*if* this) and (3) new interventions (*then* that) expected in the evolution of a given problem's natural history. Monitoring parameters are selected to measure progress, identify adverse consequences of the intervention, and identify the "next events" as early as possible. The worksheet is compiled from the interactions of comanagers and is intended to surface discrepancies between them, causing discussion for their resolution. Its use should bring about a convergence of expectations.

If the monitoring process includes parameters that are objective or that can be scaled (for instance, the rating of appetite on a scale of 1 to 4, the rating of motivational ability by patient priorities, or the rating of feeling of well-being on a scale of 1 to 10), these observations are then recorded on a chart (Form 2). This chart may then be photocopied as a means of communicating findings to other providers involved. In the sample provided, a section of the bottom of the form is reserved for narrative comments that may be necessary to clarify the coded summary. This narrative is written on the copy, leaving the original unused for future reports. In addition, the form provides a space to request a response from the addressee. A response may be requested to answer a specific question, to confirm a general concept displayed by the client or patient, or to agree or disagree with a change in management recently introduced by the other provider.

In this era of computer technology and telecommunication, multilevel information entry and transmission can be achieved for interprofessional communication networking, provided confidentiality is maintained. We have just described a paper-and-pencil process in which transmission between professional comanagers should not differ from present communication of consultation requests and responses. This process is equally applicable to electronic transmission. Such electronic transmission of shared clinical information is just beginning to be studied. Protecting clinical information is a major concern. Operational and procedural manuals with safeguarding coding systems are being developed to protect the confidentiality of clients and patients, as well as the interests of the professionals involved.

In summary, communication has been identified as a major problem in interprofessional care. An intervention has been proposed for the purpose of directing problem formation, encouraging role identification and acceptance, and reducing the time and resource barriers to communication. Electronic communication between professional team members will require greater vigilance to protect confidentiality.

CONCLUSION

Longitudinal care of clients or patients has been considered from various perspectives, with emphasis on prospective management and the adaptive needs of interprofessional team members in attending to evolving changes in patient problems. Each basic assumption was conceptually developed, relevant models were described, and application to practical clinical problems was discussed. Special attention was given to necessary role diversification for various professionals entering and leaving the collaborative effort to ensure continuity of care and effective communication among participating team members. Intervention strategies linked to the development of client social function were outlined as the foundation of multilevel and sequential integration of care management when professionals of different disciplines work together. Finally, a model of process was proposed to facilitate communication and identify incongruent expectations among collaborating providers.

REFERENCES AND RELATED READINGS

Balint, M. (1957). *The doctor, his patient and the illness*. New York: International Universities Press.

Becker, M. H., Nathanson, C. A., Drachman, R. H., and Kurscht, J. P. (1977). Mother's health beliefs and children's clinic visits: A prospective study. *Journal of Community Health, 3*, 125–135.

Berger, K. S. (1983). *The developing person through the life span*. New York: Worth.

Brody, D. S., and Larson, D. B. (1992). The role of primary care physicians in managing depression. *Journal of General Internal Medicine, 7*, 243–247.

Bronfenbrenner, U. (1979). *The ecology of human development*. Cambridge, MA: Harvard University Press.

Caplan, G. (1964). *Principles of preventive psychiatry*. New York: Basic Books.

Drinka, T. J. K. (1990). The many facets of interprofessional leadership on a long-term interdisciplinary health care team. In J. R. Snyder (Ed.), *Interdisciplinary health care teams: Proceedings of the Twelfth Annual Conference* (pp. 2–17). Indianapolis: Division of Allied Health Sciences, Indiana University School of Medicine, Indiana University Medical Center.

Driscoll, C. E., Potter, W. Z., and Rothschild, A. J. (1992). Don't overlook depression. *Patient Care, 26*, 155–188.

Ducanis, A. J., and Golin, A. K. (1979). *The interdisciplinary health care team*. Germantown, MD: Aspen Systems.

Eisenberg, L. (1992). Treating depression and anxiety in primary care: Closing the gap between knowledge and practice. *New England Journal of Medicine, 326*, 1080–1084.

Erikson, E. H. (1963). *Childhood and society*. New York: Norton.

Gerber, P. D., Barrett, J. E., Barrett, J. A., Oxman, T. E., Manheimer, E., Smith, R., and Whiting, R. D. (1992). The relationship of presenting physical complaints to depressive symptoms in primary care patients. *Journal of General Internal Medicine, 7*, 170–173.

Janis, I. L., and Rodin, J. (1979). Attribution, control, and decision making: Social psychology and health care. In G. C. Stone, F. Cohen, and N. Adler (Eds.), *Health psychology—A handbook: Theories, applications, and challenges of a psychological approach to the health care system* (pp. 487–521). San Francisco: Jossey-Bass.

Janz, N. K., and Becker, M. H. (1984). The health belief model: A decade later. *Health Education Quarterly, 11,* 1–45.

Johnson, J., Weissman, M. M., & Klerman, G. L. (1992). Service utilization and social morbidity associated with depressive symptoms in the community. *Journal of the American Medical Association, 267,* 1478–1483.

Kannel, W. B., and Sorlie, P. (1979). Some health benefits of physical activity: The Framingham study. *Archives of Internal Medicine, 139,* 857–861.

Kempe, H. C., and Helfer, R. E. (Eds.). (1980). *The battered child* (3rd ed.). Chicago: Chicago University Press.

Klaus, M. M., and Kennell, J. H. (1976). *Maternal-infant bonding.* St. Louis: Mosby.

Knesper, D. J., and Pagnucco, D. J. (1987). Estimated distribution of effort by providers of mental health services to U.S. adults in 1982 and 1983. *American Journal of Psychiatry, 144,* 883–888.

Lee, D. B., and Williams, P. T. (1984). *Multiple entry model of interdisciplinary intervention* (a lecture note). Columbus: The Ohio State University.

Lerner, R. M., Palermo, M., Spiro, A., and Nesselroade, J. R. (1982). Assessing the dimensions of temperamental individuality across the life span: The dimensions of temperament survey. *Child Development, 53,* 145–169.

LeVine, D. (1962). *A conceptual model for classification of specific social functioning by state of client functioning and by strategy of intervention* (a research framework). Tallahassee: Florida State University.

Lowther, N. B. (1991). A model of interdisciplinary care delivery. In J. R. Snyder (Ed.), *Interdisciplinary health care teams: Proceedings of the Thirteenth Annual Conference* (pp. 98–104). Indianapolis: Division of Allied Health Sciences, Indiana University School of Medicine, Indiana University Medical Center.

Mausner, J. S., & Kramer, S. (1985). *Mausner and Bahn Epidemiology: An introductory text* (2nd ed.). Philadelphia: Saunders.

McGuire, T. G., & Fairbank, A. (1988). Patterns of mental health utilization over time in a fee-for-service population. *American Journal of Public Health, 78,* 134–136.

Piaget, J. (1952). *The origins of intelligence in children.* (M. Cook, Trans.) New York: International University Press.

The Prevention Index. (1992). *Summary Report.* Emmaus, PA: Rodale Press.

Rakel, R. E., and Williamson, P. S. (1984). Use of consultants. In R. E. Rakel (Ed.), *Textbook of Family Practice* (3rd ed.). Philadelphia: Saunders.

Rapoport, L. (1965). The state of crisis: Some theoretical considerations. In H. Parad (Ed.), *Crisis intervention* (pp. 22–31). New York: Family Service Association of America.

Robertson, D. (1992). The roles of health care teams in care of the elderly. *Family Medicine, 24,* 136–141.

Starfield, B. (1985). *The effectiveness of medical care: Validating clinical wisdom.* Baltimore: Johns Hopkins University Press.

Tversky, A., and Kahneman, D. (1974). Judgment under uncertainty: Heuristics and biases. *Science, 185,* 1124–1131.

Vander Zanden, J. W. (1981). *Human development* (2nd ed.). New York: Knopf.

Wells, K. B., Hays, R. D., Burnam, A., Rogers, W., Greenfield, S., and Ware, J. E., Jr. (1989). Detection of depressive disorder for patients receiving prepaid or fee-for-service care. *Journal of the American Medical Association, 262,* 3298–3302.

CHAPTER 8

Education
for
Interprofessional Practice

R. Michael Casto, M.Div., Ph.D.

PROGRAM ASSUMPTIONS

Education for interprofessional practice should be based on educational principles that provide a foundation for exploring the opportunities available in the interprofessional context. Such a set of principles needs to be established in order to ensure that students achieve maximum benefit from their learning experiences and that all students work from the same basis. On the other hand, the principles must also be flexible enough to respond to the varying learning styles and curricular requirements of a wide range of professional education programs. The assumptions for interprofessional education that follow are designed to respond to these varying needs while at the same time maintaining the integrity of students' educational experiences.

■ *Assumption One*

Interprofessional education should be provided in areas where profession-al education programs have common or overlapping interests. As indicated in Chapter 1, increasing technological complexity has magnified the fundamental interdependence of the helping professions, an interdependence that originates in the view of the human organism as an integrated system. Health can no longer be seen as a concern separate from optimal social functioning or general well-being, as is illustrated by the case of Olga (see Chapter 10). Significant technological advances are available to the Olgas of our society, including drug therapies to save lives and maximize psychological functioning. However, in the case of Olga, there was a strong inclination among those assisting her to ignore her fundamental rights as well as her religious convictions in order to use the therapies that technological advances have made available. In all cases, professionals offering care must be prepared to respond to clients in terms of the multidimensionality of life and must recognize the importance of a holistic approach to clients' problems.

This principle expresses a commitment about the nature of interprofessional education. Such education provides an opportunity for a perspective on matters of common interest to those preparing for professional service—a perspective that is absent when professional education occurs in isolation. Interprofessional education enables us to identify questions, approach problems, and clarify issues in ways that are unavailable when we respond to the same circumstances from within the narrow confines of our professional training and experience.

The results of education in an interprofessional context should enable us to approach issues common to other professions with a breadth and depth of understanding that would otherwise be missing. This understanding should apply to both client care and the solution of complex theoretical problems and issues. Examples of areas of concern common to different professions might include communication skills, decision-making, professional socialization and values, ethical problem-solving, and client interviewing.

Additionally, knowledge and skills that enhance interprofessional practice, such as those related to group behavior and interprofessional teamwork (see Chapters 4 and 5), are the proper subject matter of our interprofessional training. We need to encourage one another—fellow practitioners, clients, students, and teachers—to develop a vision of the potential for interprofessional practice in a variety of forms (see Chapter 6); we also need the opportunity to experience a variety of models for our professional practice.

■ Assumption Two

Interprofessional education should be provided in areas where it would be in the client's or society's interest to enhance communication and cooperation between the professions. The professions may not recognize the value of interprofessional collaboration in areas in which they do not have an obvious common or overlapping interest with other professions. For example, public policy initiatives in education may seem to have little obvious relevance to the medical professions. However, educational policy may be influential in determining society's attitudes toward health in general as well as toward specific health problems.

Public policy analysis and formulation may not seem to provide an obvious opportunity for interprofessional education, especially for the helping professions, which are oriented to serving the needs of individual clients. However, skills in interprofessional collaboration may be crucial in developing policies that respond to the interests of one profession without sacrificing the goals of another.

This perspective suggests that just as the client must be viewed as an integrated system, interacting both internally and externally with many subsystems, so also must the institutions and programs that respond to human needs for education, health, and welfare be viewed holistically. In the case of the King school (see Chapter 10) narrow political goals seem to be the motive in policy decisions, whether the school ends up being closed as the administration has decided or is kept open as some favor. In either case, what is needed is a holistic vision of the community and its children, families, and businesses.

Professionals are an important ingredient in the organization of society. Their vision for society as well as for their individual clients needs to extend beyond the limits of their professional orientation. Education for interprofessional practice provides the opportunity for students to explore the common elements and interests of their professional role in society.

■ *Assumption Three*

Education for interprofessional practice should enhance both the students' knowledge of their professional area of competence and their skills and knowledge in interprofessional practice. A minimal level of professional competence and knowledge should be required of any student enrolling in an interprofessional course. Although the level of students' competence may vary, to be successful, interprofessional education requires some professional expertise as well as significant professional commitment.

The level and measure of competence may vary among the participating professions, since professional programs differ. Each professional school should determine the minimal level of competence and clinical experience it will require of students participating in interprofessional education programs. In every case, however, those establishing standards should be certain that students do not perceive opportunities in interprofessional education as a substitute for achieving professional competence.

Courses that educate students to engage in interprofessional practice should be designed both to require and to encourage professional competence. Students should be prepared within the context of the course to bring the expertise of their profession to bear on the interprofessional discussion of client problems. Courses should provide opportunities for students to explore and assess the information and experience of their profession in relation to the problems being considered. Students from the same profession should be encouraged to share their research so that each student brings to the interprofessional experience as comprehensive a view of the perspective of that student's profession as possible.

■ *Assumption Four*

Education for interprofessional practice is an essential element at all stages in professional education, including the lifelong learning programs of practicing professionals. Early exposure to the concept of interprofessional practice may be important in the process of socializing students into their professions. Research suggests that early decisions about one's profession remain influential throughout one's professional career (Simpson, 1979; Waugaman, 1988). It may be that an early exposure to the opportunities and values of interprofessional practice will have a lasting influence on students' attitudes toward professional practice.

The processes of professional socialization, developing role identity, and clarifying professional values have different outcomes for the student if they include an interprofessional dimension. As Waugaman points out (see Chapter 3), the content of the educational program, as well as its design and the particular relationship modeled by faculty members and practitioners, all play an important role in developing the student's self-understanding as a member of a profession. Role modeling by faculty members and practicing professionals is particularly important for students developing a self-identity. Interprofessional collaboration should be modeled for students both in the classroom and in their clinical experiences so that students understand and experience the intrinsic value of the interprofessional approach to practice. The case of Roger (see Chapter 10) points out the importance of professional role modeling, both for professionals themselves and for their clients.

Students educated in an interprofessional context are more articulate about the interprofessional nature of their professional practice. They are able to cite specific examples of their engagement in interprofessional practice. They enthusiastically endorse the value of interprofessional practice within their own professional self-understanding and as a benefit to their clients (Spencer, 1983). They also feel better prepared for professional practice and more stimulated once they enter professional practice. In what may be a surprising result, they have a closer identification with their own profession, are more likely to join their own professional associations, and more readily seek assistance from their associations (Harbaugh, Casto, and Burgess-Ellison, 1987, p. 144).

On the other hand, the intrinsic value of education for interprofessional practice may be more easily recognized by the experienced professional. Research suggests that people who enroll in interprofessional courses are a little older than the average student and many have had more than one career (Harbaugh, Casto, and Burgess-Ellison, 1987, p. 141). Exposure to the ambiguities and demands of clinical practice may intensify the sense of urgency professionals feel to find alternatives to their isolation, thereby increasing their receptivity to the concept of interprofessional collaboration in the care of clients. As Harbaugh points out, "an increased emphasis on interprofessional education would probably result in an even greater reliance on a cooperative and collaborative style among the professions" (Harbaugh, Casto, and Burgess-Ellison, 1987, p. 143). Such an approach to professional practice is valued by many professionals as an effective way to deliver professional services in complex cases (Kane, 1983, pp. 10–12; Allen, Casto, and Janata, 1985, pp. 103–106; Spencer, 1983, pp. 14–16).

Finally, throughout every stage in preparation for professional practice, students should be exposed to appropriate opportunities for interprofessional collaboration. Classroom activities and clinical programs should integrate interprofessional practice skills and information with other learning goals and experiences. This approach requires that faculty engaged in professional education be aware of opportunities for interprofessional interaction in the practice of their disciplines; knowledgeable about the skills required for interprofessional practice; committed to the concept of interprofessional collaboration as a substantive aspect of practicing their professions; and experienced in relating to members of other professions.

■ Assumption Five

Education for interprofessional practice moves through a progression of awareness. First, there is a need for *sensitivity* to the advantage of comprehensive rather than fragmented delivery of service. Next, there is an *openness* to the perspectives of other professions in achieving a more complete understanding of clients' needs. Then follows *engagement* in the cooperative delivery of services. Finally, what results is *cooperation* in policy formulation through shared study and implementation by professionals and their professional associations.

Students may enter the progression at any point, including a point prior to achieving any sensitivity to the advantages of an interprofessional approach. They may enroll in an interprofessional course simply because of the time it is offered, the faculty member teaching it, or their interest in the subject matter through which interprofessional collaboration is taught. Or students may approach the interprofessional education experience as seasoned professionals. Their own experience in professional practice may have led them to develop a sensitivity for the values of collaboration, but they are uncertain about how to act on this instinct. The case of Jimmie (see Chapter 10) illustrates the professional isolation that can occur in professional life and in private encounters.

Students may already have developed an openness to the perspectives of other professionals, but they would like experience in actually working with people from other professions. Students may have already been engaged in the cooperative delivery of services but want to develop further skill in this area. Or they may suspect that more lasting effects could be achieved through interprofessional collaboration but are uncertain about how to effect change.

As a process, therefore, education for interprofessional practice must provide for students with a variety of perspectives, skills, and experiences. Course goals and objectives and class activities must be designed to allow students to make optimum use of their experiences and knowledge. Theoretical and conceptual presentations must address the needs both of the student in a professional education program and of the seasoned veteran.

■ Assumption Six

Education for interprofessional practice requires the institutional commitment of funds, personnel, and physical facilities. This commitment is needed by both preprofessional and continuing education programs. Without adequate institutional support, interprofessional education has neither integrity nor continuity. Students, faculty, administrators, practitioners, funding sources, and society will come to value interprofessional education and practice in relation to the value placed on it by the institutions that train professionals and provide lifelong learning for practitioners.

The assumptions for interprofessional education just discussed provide the theoretical basis for programs that teach interprofessional collaboration as an integral part of their professional curriculum. These assumptions define and describe the essential elements of interprofessional education at both the professional and continuing education levels. They suggest a high level of commitment to theories of interprofessional collaboration, its value for professional practice, its importance within the structured curricula of professional education, and its continued influence in the lifelong learning goals of practicing professionals. A number of factors and conditions, however, are necessary to establish and sustain collaborative programs.

CONDITIONS NECESSARY FOR COLLABORATIVE PROGRAMS

A number of conditions may be necessary for collaborative work to begin and continue.[1] These conditions correlate with the assumptions about interprofessional education discussed in the preceding section. Some of the conditions are institutional or environmental in character, whereas others relate to the makeup of the team and the individual characteristics of team members. These conditions are based on the experiences of individuals and programs over a number of years. The conditions have more to do with instincts and insights than with research and facts. Although many are based on experience in

---

[1] Information in this section was developed by the author in 1990 for presentation at Temple University and at the First Annual Yukon Symposium on Interprofessional Education and Practice. It later appeared in L. M. Mauro and J. H. Woods (Eds.), *Building Bridges: Interdisciplinary Research in Child Abuse,* Philadelphia: Temple University, 1991.

an educational context, we believe they have broad applicability for any interprofessional endeavor, including practice teams in institutions and communities.

■ *Neutral Base of Operation*

Turf is the single most difficult issue to address when considering collaborative work. Professional education and practice are specialized and generally proceed with professionals in isolation from one another. We are each socialized through the process of our professional education to believe not only that we have something of value to offer our clients, but that we may have the only or at least the most valuable perspective to offer them. The longer we practice, the more entrenched we may become in this belief. These dimensions of our education discourage and inhibit us from interacting effectively with people from different professional perspectives and hamper our efforts to provide education, service, or effective policy leadership.

A neutral frame of reference for our work is essential if we are to overcome our usual instinct to protect our own turf. Where our collaborative work is located and who provides leadership and funding are important considerations in establishing this neutrality.

■ *Administrative Support*

Nothing will be accomplished through collaborative work with any consistency or for any duration without administrative support for collaboration. Scheduling meetings, developing agendas, providing housing and hospitality, observing team process, facilitating discussion, providing for evaluation and follow-up—all require administrative support that cannot be assumed to be available in the job descriptions of educators, practitioners, and policy-makers. Either real time must be available in the job descriptions of these people, or separate administrative structures must be established to facilitate collaborative practice.

■ *Shared Interest and Commitment*

There is no substitute for the shared interest and commitment of team members. Team members must hold in common not only a task, but a sense of the value of and the potential for collaboration, and must be committed to bringing that value into reality.

■ *Shared Credit*

We can make progress in a collaborative enterprise only when we are willing to give credit to the team and its sponsors. If, as independent individuals, we seek recognition for our work, our work will fail. By seeking recognition, we put ourselves in competition with others on the team and undermine the spirit of our collaborative endeavor.

■ *Shared Resources*

Sharing resources may be one of the most difficult principles to implement. Team members often do not have control over accounting for the use of existing resources. Teams need to show how resources were used in the best interest of an agency or employer. To allow those resources to be used to benefit another agency or employer does not, on the surface, seem to be in the best interest of one's own employer. But collaborative work that is developed at the expense of only one agency or group cannot be sustained. Eventually, the funding source will believe that it "owns" the team effort, a belief that will destroy the team.

■ *Partnership with the Community*

Collaborative efforts must forge genuine partnerships with the clients these efforts are designed to serve. Collaboration that involves only professionals will fall short of meeting the real needs of the people being served. Again, this point is illustrated well by the case of the King school (see Chapter 10); there, communication between the community on the one hand, and the policy-makers and professionals who made the decision to close the school on the other, seems to have broken down.

■ *Training in Collaborative Skills*

People who work in collaborative endeavors do not automatically have the requisite skills to participate in the collaborative work. Each team needs to assess the skills it will need for collaboration. Each team then needs to provide for the development and maintenance of those skills among its members. Personnel preparation programs interested in preparing their students for collaborative practice will need to provide opportunities for education in collaborative skills for students at the preservice level. Employers establishing collaborative team efforts will need to recruit new employees from educational institutions that provide appropriate interprofessional training. This text addresses one aspect of this need.

■ *Building Horizontal Bridges*

The vertical structures established in the education, practice, and policy sectors need to be bridged by collaborative work. Indeed, the main task of the collaborative enterprise is to build horizontal connections between existing vertical structures. The case of S.B. (see Chapter 10) illustrates the importance and potential for collaboration across the professional lines and structures that we have constructed for giving care and practicing our professions.

■ *Rewards*

Individuals and institutions need to be rewarded for collaborative endeavors. Criteria for promotion, salary increases, and institutional funding need to include measures of collaborative practice.

THE PARADOX OF COLLABORATION

In essence, then, these conditions for collaboration challenge our usual individual and institutional values. It is nothing short of a paradox that the less competitive we are (the less we follow our usual instinct to compete), the more competitive (in other words, effective) our collective efforts will become. The less power we have and the more power we give up, the more powerful our collaborative position will become. The more we give others credit for our work, the more credit our work will deserve. The more we shift our commitments from institutions and policies and toward our joint mission, the more commitment we will have to our institution through its mission. Our usual values are thus turned upside down in the process of carrying out collaborative work. The conditions for collaboration lead us to question existing models of professional interaction and to propose interprofessional collaboration in several forms.

RESOURCES FOR ESTABLISHING COLLABORATIVE WORK

The number of resources available for establishing collaborative work—whether in the practice, education, or policy arenas—is increasing with each passing day. What follows is intended only as a sample of the diversity and breadth of resources available to those interested in new initiatives in interprofessional education and collaborative practice. A few of these programs, like the Ohio Commission on Interprofessional Education and Practice, have been in place for a number of years. But those programs are the exception. Most of the programs identified here began in the late 1980s or early 1990s. The field is new and growing, and those engaged in it are universally optimistic about its potential for making a significant impact on the quality of life in our society.

■ *The National Consortium on Interprofessional Education and Practice*

An important effort at the national level to explore the potential for interprofessional education and collaborative practice has taken form in the National Consortium on Interprofessional Education and Practice. The National Consortium offers access to the leading helping professional and educational associations in the United States. Participating associations include the following:

American Association of Colleges for Teacher Education
American Association of Colleges of Nursing
American Bar Association
American Counseling Association
American Medical Association
American Psychological Association
Association of Schools of Allied Health Professions
Association of American Law Schools
Association of Theological Schools
Commission on Interprofessional Education and Practice
Council on Social Work Education
Hebrew Union College
National Association of Social Workers
National Council of Churches
National Education Association

The National Consortium proposes to address national needs from an interprofessional perspective by sponsoring national conferences on current issues for leaders and members of the national professional associations. It makes national professional associations aware of opportunities for improving professional services through interprofessional education and practice. The consortium is intended to stimulate the planning and implementation of interprofessional education for students and practitioners and to serve as a clearinghouse for information about models for interprofessional education and practice. It also encourages other organizations to explore programs in interprofessional education and practice, conducts research on interprofessional process, and defines issues amenable to interprofessional policy analysis.

■ *Resources for Collaborative Practice*

The availability of increased resources for the integrated delivery of human services is driven largely by funding sources encouraging or requiring more imaginative and more holistic approaches to the pressing and increasingly complex and frustrating problems of U.S. society. Available resources include literature, funding sources, and research. The following lists are not intended to be comprehensive but rather to point the way to the seminal thinking and initiatives concerning collaborative practice at the time of this writing.

LITERATURE.   The literature in the field is increasing. Useful terms for doing literature searches include *interprofessional, collaboration, interdisciplinary, multidisciplinary,* and *integrated services.* While some of the available literature is generic in nature, the vast majority relates to specific problems such as Alzheimer's disease, substance abuse, and the need for early intervention, or to specific populations such as older people.

The Education and Human Services Consortium in Washington, D.C., has published a very useful series of monographs for establishing collaborative practice. Especially helpful in this series are *Thinking Collaboratively: Ten Questions and Answers to Help Policy Makers Improve Children's Services* (Bruner, 1991) and *What It Takes: Structuring Interagency Partnerships to Connect Children and Families with Comprehensive Services* (Melaville and Blank, 1991). In *Thinking Collaboratively,* Bruner offers suggestions about how policy decisions can foster local collaboration. Melaville and Blank address how to begin collaborative work and identify the factors that affect systems and service delivery. Both publications contain excellent bibliographies.

A new journal has just begun publication in the United Kingdom under the title *Journal of Interprofessional Care.* The journal presents research and descriptive articles that address holistic approaches to the care of individuals in the community and in primary health, hospital, and other institutional settings.[2]

Since 1978, an ad hoc group of professionals and scholars from North America has been meeting annually to share their experiences and research about interdisciplinary practice in the health professions. The proceedings of this Annual Interdisciplinary Health Care Team Conference contain a wealth of information, both anecdotal and based on qualitative and quantitative research, that is of assistance to anyone interested in team development and process in health care.[3]

FOUNDATION INITIATIVES.   A number of national foundations, including the Ford Foundation, The W. K. Kellogg Foundation, The Annie E. Casey Foundation, and The Stuart Foundations, have committed significant portions of their budgets to enabling and enhancing integrated service delivery. Projects range from local initiatives that provide interprofessional care to a specific client population, to national programs aimed at the development of new policies. Additionally, numerous state and local foundations have embarked on new programs to provide integrated services in their community or region.

MODEL PROGRAMS.   Numerous model programs have been established through local initiatives using both public and private resources. One such program is the Richland County Youth and Family Regional Council of Gov-

---

[2] The journal began publication in March 1992 and is available from Carfax Publishing Company, P.O. Box 25, Abingdon, Oxfordshire, OX14, 3UE, United Kingdom.
[3] The proceedings are available from the College of Health and Human Services, Bowling Green State University, Bowling Green, OH 43403-0280.

ernments in Richland County, Ohio. This collaborative effort provides a structure to facilitate and encourage system collaboration, especially in relation to
county children and families with multiple needs. The program provides a total
family-serving system of care. It includes centralized intake for holistic family
assessment; an intensive home-based program to assist families with children at
risk of being placed out of the home as a result of abuse, neglect, emotional
problems, or a combination of these; and an intensive day treatment program
for children with emotional and behavioral problems too severe for placement
in traditional educational settings. *What It Takes* (Melaville and Blank, 1991)
describes a number of other model programs.

Another resource for identifying model programs is the National Center
for Service Integration. The center serves as a clearinghouse for information and
provides technical assistance to field-based initiatives and providers.[4]

■ *Resources for Interprofessional Education*

Increased interest in integrated service delivery has been accompanied by an
acknowledgment that professionals and administrators need special preparation
for collaborative work. A number of resources exist for establishing interprofessional education programs.

Certainly the Ohio Commission on Interprofessional Education and Practice, described in Chapter 12, has made an important and lasting contribution to
the field of interprofessional education. The cornerstone of its work has been
the preparation of professionals to work in the collaborative, integrated delivery
of human services. Much of the research and most of the curricular materials
and educational techniques have been shared with other institutions embarking
on the tedious but promising journey of providing interprofessional personnel
preparation. The Ohio Commission has been an invaluable resource for the
growth of the field and stands as a benchmark for other programs in terms of
both longevity and quality.

The work and proceedings of the Annual Interdisciplinary Health Care
Team Conference, mentioned earlier, are another major resource for interprofessional education. Numerous entries address educational and curricular issues
in interdisciplinary training. Many of the articles were generated by faculty and
others responsible for providing interdisciplinary education.

An initiative begun at the University of Washington at Seattle in 1992, to
identify the skills needed for collaborative practice among children, youth, and
families at risk, is equally important. This multiyear interprofessional effort
promises to make significant contributions to the existing knowledge base about
education for collaborative delivery of human services.[5]

Another initiative to establish university-based education for collaborative

---

[4] The center is housed at Mathtech, Inc., 5111 Leesburg Pike, Suite 702, Falls Church, VA 22041.
[5] Information on the project can be obtained from the Human Services Policy Center, University of
Washington, Seattle, WA 98195.

practice is under way at Baylor University through its college of education. Here the emphasis is on teacher preparation for interprofessional practice.[6]

Certain foundations, both national and local, have also taken the initiative to explore the need for interprofessional preservice education for collaborative practice. These foundations include many of those that have funded programs in interprofessional practice.

■ Resources for Interprofessional Policy Formulation

An arena for collaborative work that has opened up even more recently is interprofessional public policy formulation. This work has evolved through a number of different expressions. We will cite only two here.

The interprofessional policy panels developed by the Ohio Commission on Interprofessional Education and Practice are described in Chapter 9. These panels are apparently unique in a number of respects. They bring together, through voluntary associations of individuals, the intelligence of practitioners and educators to address problems of common interest. The panels do not constitute advocacy groups but are focused on problems related to the integrated delivery of human services.

Another initiative has found expression in the legislative agenda of the California General Assembly. In February 1992, Assembly Bill No. 2765 was introduced. The bill called for a collaborative effort among departments at the state level to address the training needs of professionals preparing to provide integrated human services to families and children.

CONCLUSION

During the process of writing this book, one faculty team has struggled with the paradoxes offered by the challenge of interprofessional education for collaborative practice. Each professional who hopes to engage in collaborative practice will need to accept the challenges teamwork offers and to welcome the learning and experience of other institutions and individuals.

REFERENCES AND RELATED READINGS

Allen, A. S., Casto, R. M., and Janata, M. M. (1985). Interprofessional practice. In A. S. Allen (Ed.), *New options, new dilemmas* (pp. 103–111). Lexington, VA: Lexington Books.

---

[6] Information on this program can be obtained from the College of Education, Baylor University, Waco, TX 76798.

Basuray, J. (1992). Preparing health care professionals for providing culturally congruent care: An educational framework. In J. R. Snyder (Ed.), *Interdisciplinary health care teams: Proceedings of the Thirteenth Annual Conference* (pp. 177–189). Indianapolis: Division of Allied Health Sciences, Indiana University School of Medicine, Indiana University Medical Center.

Billups, J. O., and Julia, M. C. (1987). Interprofessional education for team practice—Substance and system. In M. Brunner and R. M. Casto (Eds.), *Interdisciplinary health team care: Proceedings of the Eighth Annual Conference* (pp. 182–193). Columbus: School of Allied Medical Professions and The Commission on Interprofessional Education and Practice, The Ohio State University.

Brown, G. (1992). Problems and issues of interdisciplinarity in higher education. In J. R. Snyder (Ed.), *Interdisciplinary health care teams: Proceedings of the Thirteenth Annual Conference* (pp. 150–157). Indianapolis: Division of Allied Health Sciences, Indiana University School of Medicine, Indiana University Medical Center.

Bruner, C. (1991). *Thinking collaboratively: Ten questions and answers to help policy makers improve children's services.* Washington, DC: Education and Human Services Consortium.

Casto, R. M. (1991). An institution's experience in providing for interprofessional education and practice. In J. R. Snyder (Ed.), *Interdisciplinary health care teams: Proceedings of the Twelfth Annual Conference* (pp. 202–210). Indianapolis: Division of Allied Health Sciences, Indiana University School of Medicine, Indiana University Medical Center.

Casto, R. M. (1992). The turmoil of turf: Interprofessional collaboration in the war zone. In J. R. Snyder (Ed.), *Interdisciplinary health care teams: Proceedings of the Thirteenth Annual Conference* (pp. 198–204). Indianapolis: School of Allied Health Sciences, Indiana University School of Medicine, Indiana University Medical Center.

Casto, R. M. (In press). Inter-professional work in the USA: Education and practice. In A. Leathard (Ed.), *Going inter-professional: Working together for health and welfare.* London: Routledge.

Casto, R. M. (In press). Defining, supporting, and maintaining interprofessional education. In L. Adler and S. Gardner (Eds.), *The politics of linking schools and social services.* Bristol, PA: Falmer Publishers.

Casto, R. M., Grant, H. K., and Burgess-Ellison, J. A. (1987). Attitude changes among students engaged in interprofessional education: Further results and discussion. In M. Brunner and R. M. Casto (Eds.), *Interdisciplinary health team care: Proceedings of the Eighth Annual Conference* (pp. 305–318). Columbus: School of Allied Medical Professions and The Commission on Interprofessional Education and Practice, The Ohio State University.

Casto, R. M. and Macce, B. R. (Eds.). (1990). A model interprofessional curriculum in child abuse and neglect. *Interprofessional Education and Practice Occasional Papers* (No. 2). Columbus: The Commission on Interprofessional Education and Practice.

Casto, R. M. Nystrom, E. P., and Burgess-Ellison, J. A. (1985). Interprofessional education and attitude change: Research design and the collaborative process. In M. R. Schiller (Ed.), *Collaborative research in allied health* (pp. 51–57). Columbus: The School of Allied Health Professions, The Ohio State University.

Casto, R. M., Nystrom, E. P., and Burgess-Ellison, J. A. (1986). Interprofessional collaboration: Attitude change among students engaged in interprofessional education. In M. J. Lipetz and M. Suvada (Eds.), *Proceedings of the Seventh Annual Conference on Interdisciplinary Health Team Care* (pp. 201–216). Chicago: The Center for Educational Development, The University of Illinois at Chicago.

Cunningham, L. L., Battison, S., and Spencer, M. H. (Winter 1982). Innovations in preparation programs. *UCEA Review, XXIII* (4), 7–10.

Dewey, J. (1916). *Democracy and education: An introduction to the philosophy of education.* New York: Macmillan.

Grant, H. K., & Casto, R. M. (1987). A conceptual framework for planning interprofessional education: Is the key content or process? In M. Brunner and R. M. Casto (Eds.), *Interdisciplinary health team care: Proceedings of the Eighth Annual Conference* (pp. 194–199). Columbus: School of Allied Medical Professions and The Commission on Interprofessional Education and Practice, The Ohio State University.

Harbaugh, G. L., Casto, R. M., and Burgess-Ellison, J. A. (Spring 1987). Becoming a professional: How interprofessional training helps. *Theory into Practice, XXVI* (2), 141–145.

Hewitt, C. M. K. (1983). The ministry case as phenomenon. In D. P. Beisswenger and D. McCarty (Eds.), *Pastoral theology and ministry: Key resources, Vol. IV: Pastoral hermeneutics and ministry* (pp. 66–71). Nashville: Association for Theological Field Education.

Kane, R. A. (1983). *Interprofessional Teamwork.* New York: Syracuse University School of Social Work.

Leathard, A. (Ed.). (In press). *Going inter-professional: Working together for health and welfare.* London: Routledge.

Lyons, J. P., and Casto, R. M. (Eds.). (1990). Interprofessional education applied: Children and youth at risk—Proceedings of the Third National Leadership Symposium on Interprofessional Education and Practice. *Interprofessional Education and Practice Occasional Papers* (No. 1). Columbus, OH: The National Consortium on Interprofessional Education and Practice.

Mauro, L., Tiffany, E., and Woods, J. H. (1991). Structural components of interdisciplinary teaching: Barriers and enhancers. In L. M. Mauro and J. H. Woods (Eds.), *Building bridges: Interdisciplinary research in child abuse* (pp. 189–195). Philadelphia: Temple University, Child Welfare Training and Research Institute.

Melaville, A. I., & Blank, M. J. (1991). *What it takes: Structuring interagency partnerships to connect children and families with comprehensive services.* Washington, DC: Education and Human Services Consortium.

Melaville, A. I., & Blank, M. J. (1993). *Together we can: A guide for crafting a profamily system of education and human services.* Washington, DC: U.S. Department of Education and U.S. Department of Health and Human Services.

Queeney, D. S., and Casto, R. M. (November 1991). Collaboration among professionals of different disciplines. *The CLE Journal and Register, 37*(6), 5–18.

Schein, E. H. (1972). *Professional education: Some new directions* (Carnegie Commission on Higher Education). New York: McGraw-Hill.

Simpson, I. H. (1979). *From student to nurse.* New York: Cambridge University Press.

Spencer, M. H. (1983). *Assessing the impact of interprofessional education on the attitudes and behaviors of practicing professionals.* Unpublished Ph.D. dissertation, The Ohio State University.

Spencer, M. H. (Spring 1983). Impact of interprofessional education on subsequent practice. *Theory into Practice, XXVI,* (2), 134–140.

Waugaman, W. R. (1988). From nurse to nurse anesthetist. In W. R. Waugaman et al. (Eds.), *Principles and practice of nurse anesthesia* (1st ed.). East Norwalk, CT: Appleton and Lange.

Wilson, S. L. (1988). Improving the effectiveness of health care delivery through education. In D. T. Firestone and K. Eleanor (Eds.), *Interdisciplinary health team care: Proceedings of the Ninth Annual Conference* (p. 163). Stonybrook: State University of New York.

CHAPTER 9

Interprofessional Policy Analysis
A Model for
Public Policy Formation

Van Bogard Dunn, B.D., Ph.D.
Luvern L. Cunningham, Ed.D.

Interprofessional policy analysis is a new concept in the annals of policy development. It responds to a growing need among legislators at all levels for information about exceptionally difficult problems confronting the human community.

The disease AIDS, for example, is devastating to the people who acquire it, the families involved, and the workplaces and institutions it touches. AIDS has evoked medical uncertainties, moral and social issues, legal questions, educational policy debates, and religious controversies that fall heavily at the doorstep of the professions. Professions tend, over time, to develop intraprofessional perspectives on the problems AIDS has created. But seldom, if ever, do we structure ways that professions can address a complicated issue interprofessionally.

Interprofessional policy analysis is designed to bring the knowledge and insights of individual professions into play in the review of problems such as

This article was originally published in *Theory Into Practice*, *XXVI* (Theme issue on "Interprofessional Education") (2, Spring, 1987), pp. 129–133, and is included here with permission of the authors. © College of Education, The Ohio State University.

those AIDS produces. Leaders from the human services professions, over extended periods of time, join in intensive discussion, probing the dimensions of a problem, leading eventually to a written statement that clarifies potential policy directions for society.

POLICY ANALYSIS PANELS

Interprofessional public policy analysis at The Ohio State University developed as a part of the response of the Ohio Commission on Interprofessional Education and Practice to the interest of professional schools and associations in the state. The societal need for interprofessional public policy analysis coincided with the commission's capacity to harness the interprofessional resources of statewide networks of representatives from several professions. The intersection of those needs prompted the commission's program of policy analysis panels.

The purpose of the panels is to explore thoroughly and comprehensively social issues for which public policy is either nonexistent or inadequate. This overall purpose is implemented by addressing the following objectives: inspection and understanding of the issue's importance from intraprofessional perspectives; exploration and analysis of the issue's importance for interprofessional education and practice; preparation of a "policy-informing document" that is available to the commission constituency, policy-makers, and the general public.

The policy-informing documents of the panels are not intended as advocacy papers. They are released to policy-makers at all levels, to commission constituencies, and to the general public as intelligence documents to be used by those who read them for whatever purposes they find valuable. The papers are written in the form of model policy documents to facilitate the reader's understanding of how issues in the larger society might be understood and how appropriate legislation or policy might be drafted.

■ *Panel Makeup and Procedures*

Each panel is composed of 16 people selected from eight of the professions that have representatives on the assembly (a special extension of the commission that includes professional schools and associations from around the state). Each of the eight professions is represented on the panel by a team of two people. Eight of the panelists are recruited from the assembly representatives, with the understanding that each of those eight will recruit a professional partner who has special interest or expertise in the issue to be explored.

Recruitment of panel members is carried out by the commission staff member who has responsibility for panel support. Prospective panelists are nominated by the commission leadership, staff, and representatives of member schools and associations, so that the selection process is collegial and open. The most critical decision in the formation of a panel is the selection of a chairperson. This choice is usually made early on in the recruitment of panel membership, so that the chairperson is selected by the commission staff in consultation with the commission leadership.

The leadership of an interprofessional policy panel rotates among the members, since the life of the panel has different needs at different times. Of course, the formal leadership is fixed on one person, but the functional leadership changes as the peculiar expertise or experience of a panelist becomes relevant for a specific task.

Approximately half of a commission staff member's time is assigned to panel support. Some of this time is simply routine management of meeting details. But the heaviest time and energy commitment of the staff member is devoted to enabling and promoting the interprofessional process itself. The panels gather together all the commission's concerns and carry them forward at a high level of conceptualization and practice. The staff member is responsible for being sensitive to this process and promoting it so that the panelists experience the excitement and rewards of interprofessional reflection and action.

A graduate research assistant is also assigned to the panels. The assistant compiles bibliographies, reproduces materials, and keeps a record of all panel proceedings. This work is essential to the efficient functioning of the panels and to the development of a database for future research on the process and product. These records may provide the information base for developing a theory of interprofessional policy analysis for disseminating the idea beyond Ohio.

Although the panels are all recruited for the purpose and objectives indicated above, each has its own unique character and develops its own integrity and procedures. Generally, the members commit themselves for a 2-year period with the understanding that they will have control over the frequency of meetings, schedule of tasks, and format of the final document. The three panels now in existence have each conceived their work differently: the panel on alternative modes of reproduction is producing model legislation; the panel on health care costs is designing a grid for evaluating the outcomes of various cost-containment strategies; and the panel on family violence is cataloging educational resources, designing a model curriculum, and exploring philosophical presuppositions underlying the use, restriction, and rejection of violence. Although all the panels from the beginning focus on producing a significant policy-informing document, the documents take shape according to the vision and self-understanding of each panel.

THE PANEL EXPERIENCE

Experience in recruiting panelists confirms the judgment that professionals view interprofessional public policy analysis as challenging and rewarding. Forty-eight people have been recruited, and almost no one has refused to participate.

Not only have professionals been willing to begin the task, but they also have persevered in a remarkable way. Attendance and participation is uniformly good.

One reason for high levels of participation is that the panels provide professionals with a structure for experiencing the excitement of working closely and creatively with highly skilled people from other professions. Another reason is that the panels give professionals an opportunity to grow in their self-understanding and their own appreciation of other professionals in a process of challenge, dialogue, and mutual support. Each of the panels has developed a strong sense of identity and a fierce loyalty to the task at hand. Perhaps this experience of community in the pursuit of a common goal is what professionals find attractive and fulfilling.

It is far too early to make definitive estimates of the value of interprofessional policy analysis for the human community, but the following tentative assessment seems to be in order. First, as far as we know, the panels are unique structures for analyzing problems currently challenging our society. Second, the interprofessional membership of the panels makes possible an analysis of public issues that promises to serve the public better than the lobbying of intraprofessional organizations limited by self-interest. Third, the generation of public policy-informing documents is an innovative attempt to make the results of thoughtful discussion of crucial issues available to policy-makers before they are pressured to react to demands for quick and simple solutions to long-range, complex problems.

Public policy formulation is an ongoing process that demands the expertise and commitment of people with a high stake in improving the quality of our cooperative existence. Professionals share in responsibility for this task but have lacked a framework that would enable them to work persistently at policy issues without duplicating or competing with the efforts of other highly motivated people. The commission's experimentation with interprofessional public policy analysis may serve to provide a structural model for people in the helping professions to cooperate in the national quest for excellence. At any rate, the work of the panels to date is surely an example of how professionals are able to collaborate in giving more than lip service to the spirit of excellence in human services policy.

The raising of standards for professional practice and the constant effort to improve the quality of education in the nation's professional schools have combined to produce an unparalleled corps of professionals for serving individual needs. This concentration on responses to personal needs has not been matched by a corresponding emphasis on societal needs. Professionals represent a tremendous untapped pool of talent for creative responses to societal problems. The panels not only bring professionals together for analysis of public issues, but also teach professionals how to deepen their own understanding of those issues and train them in developing collaborative strategies for generating and improving policy. The collaborative effort enables panel members to determine what needs to be done and to help move society toward implementing the proposed action.

The panels are task oriented, but as members address their specific tasks they are required by the panels' interprofessional composition to grow in understanding of their own professional contribution, the contributions of others, the skills required for collaborative effort, and the strategies that enable professionals to influence the formulation of public policy. The panels are thus laboratories where the idea of interprofessional practice is tested, refined, and implemented. Practice is constantly subjected to rigorous theoretical examination, and theory is required to meet the acid test of practice.

Professionals are often frustrated by the routine responsibilities of daily practice. The policy panels meet the intellectual needs of such people by confronting them with new challenges, offering them opportunities to develop new interests and skills, and raising them to new levels of awareness of human and societal needs. Panel members find the interprofessional experience not only stimulating and renewing in itself but also transferable to their intraprofessional practice.

Although the panels are created for a specific task and have a limited life span, they bring into existence a network of highly skilled people who are on call as need arises in the future. The personal relationships developed and nurtured between and among panelists are life-changing and enduring. Attitudes of openness, sensitivity, commitment, and public responsibility are invaluable resources that the panels make available to the society at large and that are in place when critical problems arise.

Each panelist becomes an embodiment of and advocate for interprofessional education and practice. The commission's initial commitment to education is honored in the panels, since panelists are simultaneously teachers and students. The process of shared responsibility, mutual support, community consciousness, and common commitment creates an educational environment that enables people to achieve wholeness in the pursuit of personal and social excellence.

A THEORETICAL FRAMEWORK

A slightly altered version of Lasswell's (1971) decision phase analysis provides a framework for policy development and analysis that allows panel participants and commission leaders to visualize how their work can in fact affect policymaking. Although Lasswell's decision phases have been augmented to some extent, they provide the essential dimensions that frame the commission's work. These phases may also be useful in the future development of interprofessional policy oversight services.

Lasswell's phases are intelligence, promotion, prescription, invocation application, termination, and appraisal (see also Cunningham, 1986). The phases convey a sense of linearity but are not intended as discrete steps in policymaking. In the hectic, day-to-day unfolding of legislative decisions, the phases lose their distinctiveness. For the purpose of policy analysis, however, they have value.

The commission has added a phase called initiation, the activity that starts or ignites a sequence of events leading to a legislative or administrative decision. To place the initiation phase in context, the discovery that a sixth-grade child in the community has AIDS could stimulate the commission to form a panel to develop policy concerning the problems created by this disease.

Brief descriptions of the use of the phases by the commission follow. Thus far, the first four phases (initiation, intelligence, promotion, and prescription) have been useful to the commission. The remaining four phases (invocation, application, termination, and appraisal) are germane to interprofessional policy oversight, a potential future service.

■ *Initiation*

The commission seeks proposals for policy panel work. Professional associations, professional schools and colleges, commission members, and leading practitioners are among those invited to nominate policy areas for consideration. Through its assembly, the commission determines which policy problems to address.

■ *Intelligence*

Following their formation, the policy panels proceed to gather information about the problem from many sources. Over time, the members sift through data from their own professions plus contributions from other professions, augmented by information of other kinds that was not generated by the professions themselves. Lengthy discussions, sifting and sorting, advancing policy ideas, and similar activities take place, leading eventually to policy-informing papers.

■ *Promotion*

Promotion is the term Lasswell (1971) uses to mean getting the word out. It involves a combination of informing and elevating awareness about a given problem's seriousness and the importance of addressing, through legislation or administrative action, the issues the problem creates. The commission disseminates its policy-informing papers directly to legislators and other public officials as well as to professionals through their associations. The commission also informs legislative leaders of its work while it is under way so that those leaders can anticipate the arrival of papers that may be important in future legislative sessions.

■ *Prescription*

Prescription is the actual adoption of a policy or law or the issuance of an executive order or another form of administrative decision. The policy panel members stand ready to explain their perspectives to those who might seek clarification or want further information. They do not, and the commission does not, advocate any one perspective.

The remaining decision phases (invocation, application, termination, and appraisal) are applicable to policy oversight and may, in the future, become additional policy panel responsibilities. Policy oversight is described in the next section in general terms, rather than phase by phase.

■ *Potential for Policy Oversight*

Policy oversight is the systematic monitoring of the effectiveness of given laws or policies—another difficult responsibility borne by public bodies of all kinds, such as boards, trustees, councils, commissions, and legislatures. Individual professions, through their practitioner communities, have windows on the world that allow them to offer data, or at least informed impressions, concerning the effectiveness of a given policy, law, rule, or regulation.

Interprofessional collaboration in the design of policy appraisal mechanisms could yield rich information about policy effectiveness that could then be synthesized and made available to policy bodies. The professions, through their professional associations, are able to collect data from practitioners efficiently. Such data, aggregated profession by profession, could then be analyzed interprofessionally through policy panels in much the same fashion that the Ohio interprofessional policy panels have worked on generating new policy proposals. The structural approaches would be similar but with more specific data-gathering tasks expected of the professional associations to meet policy oversight needs.

Conclusion

Interprofessional policy analysis has considerable potential. Experimentation at The Ohio State University is opening new ground in both the concept and the practice of policy development. Intelligent examination of complex policy problems by thoughtfully constituted groups of professionals can meet a serious legislative need.

Legislators, especially at the state level, have assistance from staff members and legislative resource bureaus to help them sort out the difficult issues they face. But as useful as these resources are, legislators are not equipped to examine questions of extraordinary complexity such as those the Ohio in-terprofessional policy panels have faced.

These problems contain ethical questions, issues of justice, matters of medical interest, and often issues concerning education and rehabilitation; these problems affect individuals, nuclear and extended families, coworkers, and employers. Gathering the intelligence and generating the analyses needed require the contribution of professional experts from many fields. Moreover, the joint and collaborative focus of attention on such matters produces, in the long run, a richer, stronger, more reliable analysis.

REFERENCES AND RELATED READINGS

Cunningham, L. L. (1986). Computers and educational governance. In J. A. Culbertson and L. L. Cunningham (Eds.), *Microcomputers and education* (Pt. 1) (88th Yearbook of National Society for the Study of Education, pp. 193–215). Chicago: University of Chicago Press.

Lasswell, H. D. (1971). *A preview of policy sciences.* New York: American Elsevier.

PART 4

Resources

Tools for Interprofessional Care and Collaborative Practice

CHAPTER 10

Case Studies

We invite each reader to identify from his or her own personal and professional perspective the practice-related and ethical issues raised by each case found in this chapter. Following each case are questions and activities examining the issues about practice and ethics raised by the case. These questions are to be discussed and studied first from a professional perspective. Comparisons of these perspectives among professions are encouraged. The same questions can then be used to analyze issues from an interprofessional perspective.

A discussion about the use of case study methodology in interprofessional courses appears in Chapter 12.

OLGA

Police brought Olga, a 67-year-old white female, into the emergency room of a general hospital late one cold January night. She had been found wandering around downtown during a light snow at 2:30 a.m. An examination revealed multiple bruises and scabs covering her body and an acute infection of her right arm. Further examination revealed symptoms of uncontrolled diabetes, a diagnosis verified by examining the patient's records.

The patient was able to give her name and to generally identify where she was. After her arm was treated she asked to be released to go home. On questioning she was unable to give her address, but claimed that she owned a home and could find her way there without any problem if released. She also refused medication, claiming that her church taught that drugs were bad for people.

Because of the concerns of the emergency room physician who examined Olga, she was assigned a room and asked to stay until the morning. She made no attempt to resist or leave, and slept well until morning. In the morning, again at the insistence of the examining physician, she was seen by a psychiatrist, who was asked to evaluate the possibility of committing Olga to the short-term state mental hospital located in the same community. The hospital chaplain also visited her and discovered that she came from a neo-Pentecostal background.

The psychiatric examination revealed chronic undifferentiated schizophrenia with some delusional ideation. The patient was definitely not a threat to others and not suicidal. On the other hand, she appeared incapable of caring for her immediate medical needs. She also seemed incapable of meeting her other needs. The psychiatrist certified her as committable and recommended short-term hospitalization to stabilize her condition.

Olga was informed of the recommendation and of her right to counsel. She asked to see a lawyer and was interviewed by one the following day. During the interview she stated her strong opposition to hospitalization and her desire to be discharged. She claimed that she had been hospitalized earlier and had found it unpleasant; she also continued to state her opposition to medication. During the preceding 2 days she had been given regular injections of insulin over her protests, but without her physical resistance. Examination of her medical records by her lawyer also revealed that she had been given 25 mg Thorazine, twice daily, ground up in her food without her knowledge.

Olga was transferred to the state mental hospital 2 days after having been brought to the emergency room. At that time, a thorough social investigation took place, which revealed that she had been hospitalized three times within the previous 5 years for periods of 1 to 3 months. She owed the state $4,800 for previous hospitalizations and had made no payments. Her last hospitalization had occurred 15 months previously. After 5 days in the hospital she was discharged to a nursing home, which she left after 3 days.

The social investigation also revealed that she did indeed own a small two-bedroom frame house in an older part of town, which she had inherited from her parents 15 years previously. A visit there found the house occupied by a 60-year-old male, Bill, who was receiving SSI disability payments and claimed to be Olga's cousin. He claimed to be concerned about Olga's whereabouts and asked that she be returned home. The house was filthy and in bad repair. Roaches were plainly visible during the day, litter and garbage were strewn throughout the house, and appliances and fixtures were covered with grime.

Olga had a joint bank account with Bill, which had been opened 6 years earlier. Her social security check was deposited directly into the account. Most recent withdrawals had been made by Bill in small amounts. Records at the general hospital emergency room revealed that Olga had been admitted by Bill 6 months earlier with a sprained ankle and cuts and bruises. Both Olga and Bill refused to discuss the cause of the injuries.

STUDENT ACTIVITY

1. Identify the issues for members of your profession in providing for the care of Olga.
2. Discuss what further information, if any, you need in order to respond to her needs.
3. Explore the relationship between Olga's diagnosis of schizophrenia and her diabetes.
4. Identify which other professionals you would need to consult in order to develop a comprehensive response to Olga's needs.
5. In consultation with other professionals, develop a collaborative plan for the care of Olga.

FOR FURTHER DISCUSSION AND STUDY

1. What ethical questions does this case raise for members of your profession? For the hospital? For the lawyer?
2. What are Olga's rights upon entering the hospital?
3. What are the hospital's responsibilities to Olga? To the community?
4. What ethical conflicts arise in dealing with a client of marginal competency?
5. Should the lawyer contact other professionals in order to assure fair and necessary care for Olga, and if so, which professionals should be contacted?
6. Can treatment be forced on a competent client? An incompetent client?

ROGER (PART 1)

Roger, a 33-year-old Hispanic male, teaches history in a conservative private high school in a small midwestern town. Roger is gay, but in the last year has been virtually celibate, only occasionally having relations with Michael, his old and dear friend. Roger has been grieving about the end of his long-standing but very well-concealed relationship with Jay, which broke up a year ago. Jay had completely renounced being gay and refused even to speak to Roger or to any of his old friends. Jay had married Peggy, an elementary school teacher who knew nothing of his past.

In the winter, Roger developed what seemed to be a very bad chest cold. He consulted Dr. Levy, his regular physician, who had known of Roger's sexual orientation and relationship with Jay for several years. Dr. Levy diagnosed Roger as having pneumonia and hospitalized him immediately. In the hospital, further tests revealed that Roger had P. Carinii pneumonia. Blood tests for HIV (the AIDS antibody) were also completed and were positive. Dr. Levy told Roger that he was HIV-positive and indeed had developed AIDS.

Because he had never before cared for an AIDS patient, Dr. Levy consulted an older colleague, Dr. Richards, about treatment. He and Dr. Richards discussed the course of treatment. Dr. Richards then indicated that because he had recently had some health problems, he would rather not participate in treating Roger or even enter his room. Dr. Levy was surprised and distressed at this attitude but did not pursue the matter any further.

In counseling Roger about his illness, Dr. Levy told him about the importance of informing present sex partners and practicing safe sex. Roger said he had no present sex partners. Dr. Levy then said he should tell past partners so they could be tested. Roger said he would tell Michael, who probably was the one who infected him. Roger said that he and Jay, however, were no longer on speaking terms and that anyway their relationship had ended a year ago. Dr. Levy told Roger that the incubation period was in some cases very long and that Jay could very likely be infected. Roger said that even so, it would do no good to tell Jay, since he couldn't do anything about being infected.

Dr. Levy was very troubled by all this. He knew that Jay had gotten married and that if he was infected, he could very well infect his wife. Dr. Levy had no personal or professional relationship with either Jay or Peggy (Peggy was a second-grade school teacher in the local elementary school). Dr. Levy took very seriously his duty to respect Roger's privacy. Yet he knew that even if Jay was infected, Peggy might not yet be, and he felt that he might be in a position to protect her from serious harm.

When Roger's condition improved, Dr. Levy broached the subject again, stressing the danger Peggy might be facing. Besides the medical risks, he was concerned about possible reactions from the community, since Peggy taught at the local school. Roger was sympathetic, but still refused to contact Jay. Roger said that if Jay did test positive for the virus, he was the sort to blame Roger and to leak information about Roger's sexual orientation to his colleagues at the school, which would undoubtedly cost him his job. Dr. Levy did not doubt this, but he remained troubled about what, if anything, he should do.

STUDENT ACTIVITY

1. Discuss the case in a collaborative group.
2. Identify the issues this case raises for your profession.
3. Discuss the legal obligations and ethical responsibilities of Dr. Levy, Dr. Richards, and Roger.

4. Identify the legal responsibilities of your profession in your state with respect to confidentiality, the legal requirement to report cases of HIV infection, and the requirement to inform sexual partners that they may have been infected.
5. Discuss the "moral" duty to inform in this case.
6. Identify the resources in your community that would be available to clients in circumstances similar to those of Roger, Jay, and Michael.
7. Identify the HIV educational resources available to professionals in your community.

ROGER (PART 2)

Dr. Levy soon encountered another ethical dilemma. Michael came to see him, Roger having told him of his diagnosis. Michael said he was sexually active, though not with any special person, and wanted counseling about safe sex practices. Michael also wanted to have a complete physical. However, Michael did not want to have the test to determine whether he was HIV-positive. He said that it would upset him too much if he tested positive and that he just didn't want to know. Dr. Levy told Michael that it wasn't fair for him to know that he was at high risk and to continue to have sex—even "safe sex"—without learning his actual status and then, if positive, informing sex partners.

Michael said that he would indeed feel guilty if he knew he was HIV-positive and didn't inform sex partners, but he also knew that he'd be treated like a leper if he did inform them. Anyway, the issue was moot, because he didn't want to know his antibody status, and the primary reason he didn't want to know was that the knowledge would be too traumatic for him to deal with.

Sadly, the dilemma about informing Jay soon became moot, because he likewise became ill. After Dr. Sullivan, Jay's personal physician, diagnosed him as HIV-positive, Jay told his wife about his past. The diagnosis came at a dreadful time, because Peggy, a devout Roman Catholic, was 4 months pregnant. Moreover, though feeling absolutely fine and without any symptom of illness, she tested HIV-positive. Her infection meant that her baby would be at some risk of developing AIDS, although that result was by no means certain. Jay and Peggy, in great distress, consulted Reverend McLaughlin, their parish priest, about what they should do.

This being a small town, Jay's illness soon became public knowledge. Some of the parents of children in Peggy's second-grade class developed a petition saying they did not want their children exposed to someone who could carry AIDS. These parents argued that even though they knew there are no documented cases of AIDS being spread by casual contact, the disease is so lethal that they did not want to take even the slightest chance of their children being exposed.

STUDENT ACTIVITY

1. Identify the new issues the information about Jay, Peggy, and Michael raises for members of your profession.
2. What other professionals would you need to consult to develop a collaborative approach to caring for Jay? Peggy? Michael?
3. Develop a collaborative plan for each client in the case.

FOR FURTHER DISCUSSION AND STUDY

1. What ethical issues does this case raise for members of this small community? Has confidentiality been violated in this case?
2. When should testing for the HIV virus be recommended?
3. Under what conditions can a professional refuse to provide services for a client? Do members of your profession have a moral responsibility to provide care? A legal duty?
4. How could members of your profession assist the community in resolving these issues?
5. How could a collaborative approach to the resolution of these community issues be used to assist in their resolution?
6. What public policy issues does this case raise?
7. What contribution could members of your profession make to the exploration of these policy issues?
8. Could an interprofessional approach to these policy questions be useful in their exploration? If so, how?

JIMMIE

Jimmie, 14 years old, lives with his parents in a suburb of a large urban area. He is an active, bright high school freshman. Recently, his father's brother came to live with them. He is 35 and unmarried.

You live next door to Jimmie and his family. Jimmie enjoys stopping by to visit and talk with you about your work and other interests. He enjoys talking with you about his plans for the future, going to college, and making a choice of a profession. He often confides in you and seeks your advice about "teenage problems." He often talks about how much he enjoys having an adult friend he can trust.

Lately, Jimmie has been acting very quiet and withdrawn. You ask if something is bothering him. Jimmie breaks down and starts talking in a sobbing voice. While listening to him, you learn that he is feeling embarrassed. His uncle has made Jimmie do some horrible things—undress in front of him, take showers with him, let him fondle and kiss Jimmie's genitalia, and talk about having sex. Jimmie is really scared of his uncle. Jimmie told his father, but his father would not listen. He said it was impossible for his brother to do anything like this. Jimmie does not know what else to do. He has been trying to ignore his uncle but that is very hard to do. Jimmie is frightened and upset, and he wonders what he should do now.

STUDENT ACTIVITY

1. Identify and discuss the issues this case presents for members of your profession.
2. Identify which professionals would be of assistance in developing a collaborative plan of care to meet Jimmie's needs.
3. With your colleagues from other professions, develop a collaborative plan for responding to Jimmie.

FOR FURTHER DISCUSSION AND STUDY

1. What are the responsibilities and obligations of your profession for reporting suspected child abuse? If you decide to report, should you tell Jimmie that you are going to make the report?
2. Are your personal responsibilities different from your legal obligations?
3. Are you responsible in this case as a private citizen or as a professional? How do you decide?
4. Should you refer Jimmie to another professional or attempt to offer services yourself?

JESSICA

Jessica Jones, a 54-year-old woman, is in the Interprofessional Family Practice Outpatient Clinic for a 6-week check on her fractured right leg (fibula). The fracture occurred when she fell down a flight of stairs in her home. The leg was set through a closed reduction and was placed in a cast for 4 weeks. After the cast was removed, physiotherapy was instituted for 2 weeks.

The nurse, while preparing Jessica for examination by Dr. Jack Anson, the physician, asks how things are going. Jessica, also a registered nurse, replies, "I'm pleased about the progress of my leg. It's the other problems that I have right now that are giving me concern." The nurse inquires further, and Jessica discloses that her husband, George, was arrested a week ago for driving while intoxicated. She expresses her concern about his drinking and the embarrassment it is causing the family. Asked how George was reacting to the situation, Jessica replies, "He's not concerned at all. He called one of his attorney friends, who is working to have the charge reduced to reckless operation."

Jessica and George, married for 30 years, have two grown children and one grandchild, Peter, age 9. Peter is living with his grandparents for this school year because his parents are on a 12-month overseas assignment with the government. George, a successful thoracic surgeon, has had a good practice for 25 years. He has taken an active role in the community and is a deacon in the church.

The nurse continues talking with Jessica and asks whether Jessica has talked with her husband about her concern. "Many times," she replies. "In fact, Dr. Anson himself spoke to George about his drinking two years ago. About that time, George and I were separated and his drinking increased. When Jack, a friend of George, brought up his drinking, George laughed and said he was worrying too much." Jessica goes on to say that she feels very discouraged about the situation. The nurse asks Jessica if George or she have ever talked with their pastor about the problem. She indicates that she has, but he has not.

When asked how Peter is adjusting to living with them, Jessica tells the nurse that he is a delight to both of them. George is very fond of Peter and was looking forward to having Peter live with them for the year. However, further conversation reveals that, initially, Peter was doing well in his new school and his grades were good. But recently, his teacher has noted that Peter's grades have slipped and that he seems somewhat withdrawn and preoccupied. Further, he has been involved in two fights on the playground in the last month and expresses reluctance some mornings to go to school.

Jessica says that she has been trying to spend more time with Peter, who seems very concerned about her leg injury. During one talk, Peter told Jessica that he is scared of Grandpa because he "acts funny." At times he is pleasant, then becomes angry with Peter for no apparent reason. Jessica tells Peter to be patient with Grandpa, that he has been very busy at the hospital.

The nurse tells Jessica that Dr. Anson will see her shortly and is about to leave the room when Jessica says, "There's one more thing about this situation that is very disturbing. I know I told you and Dr. Anson that I fell down the steps and broke my leg, but that's not exactly how it happened. The night I broke my leg, George had been home all evening and apparently had been drinking. I came home and found him in an irritable mood. We began to argue and George became agitated. My fall occurred because George pushed me out of the way as he went to his room. The frightening part is that George doesn't remember it at all. In fact, when I told him what happened, he felt terrible and couldn't imagine that he could have pushed me."

STUDENT ACTIVITY

1. You are a member of the interprofessional team in the Family Practice Clinic. This information about Jessica and George Jones is brought to you and your fellow team members at your weekly team meeting. From the perspective of your profession, identify the client in this case and the recommendations you would make.
   Discuss this case with your colleagues from other professions and develop a collaborative plan for the client.

FOR FURTHER DISCUSSION AND STUDY

1. What scope of care do Jessica, Peter, George, and the family need?
2. What ethical questions does this case raise for the nurse in the case? For members of your profession?
3. Who is responsible for reporting an impaired professional? How do you decide when you should report an impaired colleague to the appropriate authorities? Should Jessica be encouraged to report George?
4. Is an intervention appropriate in this case? If so, who should initiate it?
5. What avenues of assistance are available to impaired professionals and their loved ones?
6. How would a nurse approach this case in a collaborative manner? A member of your profession?
7. Should the school be contacted to inform them about Peter's special needs at this time? Who should make the contact?

S.B.

S.B., a male infant, was born August 1984, the result of an uncomplicated term pregnancy and a 2-hour labor following pitocin induction. APGAR scores were 7 at birth and 9 at 5 minutes. Infancy was uneventful except for mother's observation of head-banging behavior. S.B. suffered a mild concussion in an auto accident at age 2.

His parents reported moderate frustration in disciplining S.B. beginning at age 4, which was seemingly due to his not learning from previous attempts at discipline. They also noted a repetition of small accidents, as though previous incidents did not modify future behavior. He did not complete simple play activities as he flitted from one activity to another. He usually got distracted to other activities when assigned even simple chores, especially those requiring a sequence of tasks.

In third grade the teacher reported that S.B. was fidgety and out of his seat frequently and that he did not complete his desk work. Mild external noises were distracting.

A review of his medical history revealed frequent benign recurrences of abdominal pain. It was noted that he had not required training wheels in learning to ride a two-wheel bike. He is now 8.

STUDENT ACTIVITY

For each profession, consider how best to initiate collaborative interaction as we follow up on the case.

1. You are S.B.'s third-grade teacher. What classroom action would you take? How would you initiate further study? What are your expectations for further participation in managing S.B.?

2. You are the school psychologist. The teacher has discussed S.B.'s classroom behavior with you. How would you respond?

3. You are S.B.'s physician. At the preschool exam, you noticed S.B. playing with the instruments and other objects in the examining room in a manner devoid of curiosity. Your receptionist has commented about his disruptive behavior in the waiting room. How would you initiate further study of S.B. and involve others in the process?

4. You are the local prosecuting attorney. A complaint has been filed against S.B. by a neighbor. The neighbor alleges that S.B. set a fire in the neighbor's garage. What action, if any, are you required to take by law? What is your response to the complaint?

5. You are the lawyer for S.B.'s parents. They called you following a threat by the neighbors to sue for damages caused by the fire in their garage. The neighbors claim a right to compensation not only for the damaged garage, but for the damage caused by other less destructive acts of S.B., such as picking their flowers and digging in their lawn. They also claim they are entitled to compensation for the psychological distress caused by S.B.'s acts as well as the physical damage. The neighbors have agreed, however, not to sue if S.B. is removed from the neighborhood. What would your response be? As a lawyer, are you acting as a mediator or an advocate? Are these roles competing or complementary?

6. You are the social worker at the local mental health clinic. Mrs. B. has come to the clinic seeking help in handling S.B.'s discipline problems. She tells you all his teachers have had similar problems. How would you proceed?

7. You are the B. family's pastor. One of your Sunday school teachers reports to you that S.B. is disruptive in Sunday school. How would you respond?

8. You are the coach of the little league team and S.B. is your left fielder. You are also the psychologist at the mental health clinic, though S.B. and his family have never been your clients. You notice he plays by himself off to the side of the other players. When he goes to the field he plays around in his area and watches activities off the field. What would you do?

9. You are the school nurse. S.B. is unable to respond appropriately when you attempt to administer a vision screening test using the eye chart. What would your response be?

10. You are a nutritionist who has been consulted by the B. parents. They would like advice about the benefits of various dietary approaches to

ameliorating symptom patterns similar to those displayed by S.B. How would you respond to their inquiry?

FOR FURTHER DISCUSSION AND STUDY

1. What information in the case is not clear to you?
2. What other information would you need to know from the perspective of your profession in order to prepare yourself to participate in an interprofessional discussion of a treatment plan for S.B.?
3. Would it be helpful to develop a profile for S.B. that would span the time of his life? If so, how would you use such a profile? How would you go about developing it? Where should such a profile be maintained? How would access to the profile be controlled?
4. What are the ethical issues raised when professionals seek access to the records of other professionals regarding a particular client? How should such access be regulated?

SARAH

Identifying Information and Reason for Seeking Service

Sarah is a divorced female in her early 30s who presented herself at the Guidance Center for help in resolving her feelings about Sam, a man with whom she has had a love relationship for 3 years. Sam has a drinking problem, which he acknowledges on occasion. He has been drinking and smoking marijuana for more than 15 years.

Sarah lives in the small home she received in the divorce settlement and maintains custody of her two children, Mark, age 11, and June, age 8. Sam stays with the family much of the time but resides with his parents. He is also divorced. Sarah and her husband negotiated a dissolution in 1985, and she met Sam just prior to her husband's leaving. The relationship with the ex-husband is satisfactory most of the time—he pays child support and the mortgage on the home, and he spends every other weekend with the children. The relationship with Sam is not satisfactory. Although they are very much in love, the enjoyable times together are fleeting and are being replaced by much intense conflict and turmoil. Both Sarah and Sam love the children, but when she is upset she is impatient with them, and, on occasion, Sam makes nasty, cutting remarks to one or the other of them.

Sarah works part-time at a local bank branch, where she brings in perhaps half the family income. She was initially resentful at having to work outside the home at all, but Alanon has helped her handle the resentment. She is bright and articulate, but unsure of herself in many areas of her functioning.

At the time of the first appointment she was very teary, displaying a considerable amount of self-pity and placing herself in a position to have only limited joy.

Sam is employed for even fewer hours a week than Sarah; he works as a musician, giving guitar lessons part-time and playing with different groups that entertain in small bars and cafés. He has reluctantly attended some AA meetings in the past and has been seeing a local psychiatrist for weekly psychotherapy for the past 2 years. He also is bright and articulate and presents a very self-assured, if not arrogant, stance regarding the handling of his own life.

Family History

Sarah remembers her childhood with both sadness and resentment. She is the youngest of two children born into a blue-collar family from a small town. Her father had a drinking problem and was not a particularly good provider. She remembers him as a kind and quiet man, nonetheless, and was upset with how her mother nagged at and berated him. Her father died of a stroke several years ago, but she remains in contact with her mother by letter and telephone. Sarah's mother and married brother, who now has a drinking problem, live next door to one another in Montana.

Sam's youth was reported to be uneventful, as he was reared in a family that was very close and always did things together. Sam was also the youngest of two children, his brother being only 2 years older. Sam's father owns and operates a machine shop, and his mother remains a homemaker, helping the father in the office only on occasion. As mentioned earlier, Sam now lives at home and has done so since he was divorced. His parents pay for his weekly psychotherapy as well as for other expenses that he incurs. The parents are active members of a very fundamentalist Baptist Church and do not consume any alcohol. They feel even more strongly about not consuming alcohol since Sam's brother was killed 3 years ago when he drove drunk into an embankment during the early morning hours. They continue to plead with Sam not to drink.

STUDENT ACTIVITY

1. Identify the client in this case and explain your reasons for this choice.
2. Identify the ways professionals might work together in the treatment of this client.
3. Identify the professions that would be helpful in developing a plan for addressing the concerns raised in this case.
4. Identify the issues that need to be addressed in treatment from the perspective of each profession on the team.
5. Develop a collaborative plan for the client in this case.

FOR FURTHER DISCUSSION AND STUDY

1. Neither Sarah nor Sam attend church. How can spiritual issues be addressed?
2. What role can education about alcoholism and chemical dependency—the family illness—play for the family? Who might benefit by education and from what professionals?
3. What other resources might be available for this family?

KING JUNIOR HIGH SCHOOL

In the moments following the closing of the cafeteria line, Willis Bradshaw joked pleasantly with the lunchroom staff. He was proud of them. They had converted a trouble spot into a place of pride. King Junior High School, 5 years ago, was the pits, or so it was described. Parents, students, teachers, administrators—anyone who was aware of the school system—knew about King and its problems.

But that is all different now. The changes began with the appointment of Mr. Bradshaw, an ambitious young black administrator, as principal. Bradshaw sought the King job when few others would even consider it. Superintendent Frank Wallace had to be convinced at the time that Bradshaw was the person for King. Although he recommended Bradshaw's appointment, he was nervous about Bradshaw's civil rights activism in the 1960s and early 1970s. Wallace feared that conservative board members would vote down his recommendation. To his surprise, his recommendation was passed without opposition or even discussion. And Bradshaw had certainly vindicated their confidence in him. Bradshaw had always known of Wallace's initial skepticism about him. But Bradshaw's leadership had erased all doubts.

Bradshaw was tough but fair. He held high standards for King and for everyone there, blacks and whites alike. Students soon found that no one could run any games on the new principal. Teachers who were lazy or marginal soon got out. A spirit of achievement gradually replaced essentially goalless behavior, high absenteeism, conflict, and the near chaos of previous years.

Willis Bradshaw, now back in his office, glanced at the correspondence and messages lying so orderly on his desk. Mrs. Barnes was very efficient, a superb school secretary. She was a major factor in the overall improvement of the school. She was the first contact that many people had with King. Courteous, warm, businesslike, she converted the office into another King asset. It had been poorly managed, inefficient, disorderly; but not now. Mrs. Barnes, like Bradshaw, expected high performance and she got it.

The telephone note on top had been marked "urgent" in red and underlined. Mr. Bradshaw buzzed Mrs. Barnes immediately: "Edna, what can you

Used with the permission of Luvern L. Cunningham, Ed.D.

tell me about the superintendent's call?" Mrs. Barnes replied, "Well, I don't have much. Marilyn said that Dr. Wallace had to see you this afternoon. It's about the citizens' report on school closings and a story that is likely to be in tonight's paper."

"Okay, Edna, thanks. Get Dr. Wallace for me?"

"Willis, thanks for getting right back to me. I need to see you as soon as you can get down here. The Citizens' Committee is recommending that we close King next year. I thought we had headed that off, but something happened. What is worse, it's going to be in tonight's paper, even before it goes to the board." Mr. Bradshaw replied, "I'll be right there. Should I bring Herb Smith, if I can get him? This is something the PTA president ought to be in on." There was a pause, then Wallace said, "Sure. Maybe he can help. I'll have Samantha Gregg and Homer Shaughnessy here, too. Come right to the boardroom."

Bradshaw and Smith shook snow off their coats, hung them in the corner, and settled into empty places. Copies of the Citizens' Committee report were being examined by the others already there. The exchange of greetings was short as everyone turned the pages and scribbled notes hastily. After 5 minutes, Superintendent Wallace broke the silence.

"Thanks for coming on short notice. Mr. Smith, I'm especially grateful to you for leaving your office, midafternoon. I would not have convened this meeting if I had not considered this matter to be important. At about 11:00 this morning, Walter Granger and Barbara Owens dropped off the ad hoc Citizens' Committee report on school closings. We had expected it in about 10 days, but as they explained, they were finished and wanted us to have it as soon as possible. They volunteered too that copies had been given to the media. I understand that radio and TV news programs have carried stories about the report. And no doubt, tonight's *Argus* will give generous coverage to it.

"As you may know by now, the committee reversed itself on us in one important respect. They recommend closing King. When we last talked with Walter Granger and Barbara Owens, cochairpersons of the Committee, they assured us that if a junior high were to be considered for closing it would be Roosevelt. Granger and Owens, to their credit, told me of the change this morning. But they had little to offer in the way of explanation other than that the downtown development commission wants the King site for business expansion.

"Samantha and Homer, my assistants, have read the entire report. In a minute, I'll have them summarize it for us. But before they do, do either of you have any questions or comments?"

Mr. Bradshaw fanned the pages of the report, sat rigid, his eyes hostile. "Those SOB's, they're doing it to us again. King is a damn good school. Everyone in this room knows that. It's a good school, better than Roosevelt. Sure our building is old, but it's solid, and it's a symbol for blacks in this town. Bulldoze King down and you're emasculating our spirit. If the board accepts this, there will be one hell of a fight." Herb Smith joined Bradshaw in his attack upon the recommendation, "Willis is right. This will not go down easy. In fact, this will not go down at all. I came back to this town when I finished law school. My kids are in the public schools, including King. Willis Bradshaw has made King into a good school. And it is good for the 25 percent who are white as well as for blacks."

Wallace looked grim. He said, "I know how you feel. I feel the same way. Although this Citizens' Committee was not appointed by the board, I thought we were working hand in hand with the committee, especially the cochairpersons."

Marilyn, the Superintendent's secretary, entered the boardroom quietly. Dr. Wallace noticed her and paused. "The editor of the *Argus* is on the phone. Do you want to talk with him now?" she asked.

STUDENT ACTIVITY

1. Identify the power issues in this case.
2. Identify the equity issues in this case.
3. Identify the justice issues in this case.
4. Discuss the opportunities this case presents for collaborative problem-solving and decision-making.
5. Identify who should be included in seeking a collaborative solution to the problems raised in this case.

FOR FURTHER DISCUSSION AND STUDY

1. How do *you* define power, equity, and justice? How does *your profession* define power, equity, and justice?
2. What are comparable scenarios of this case in other professions?
3. What ethical concerns does this case raise?
4. In what ways does this case reinforce your stereotypes of education as a profession?
5. In what ways does this case challenge your stereotypes of education as a profession?

GINNY

Virginia (Ginny) B. is a 67-year-old woman living in a nursing home. She has Alzheimer's disease. She and her husband, Roger B. (age 70) have three children. Two of their children, Peggy S. (age 36 and married with two daughters, age 11 and 14), and Charles (age 45), are still actively involved in the lives of their parents. Ginny was first diagnosed with Alzheimer's disease by a neurologist in 1975. In 1983, a second opinion confirmed the initial diagnosis.

Mr. and Mrs. B. resided on an 80-acre family farm and had three children: one son and two daughters. Mrs. B., as a young woman, attended Capital U., studying education and religion. She was prized by her family as a wife and mother—loving, affectionate, and warm—and as a wonderful homemaker, talented as a seamstress, cook, and Sunday school teacher. Mr. B., who had been employed for 30 years at the Defense Construction Supply Center, retired at age 55 and "came home" to build their dream home on the farm. Though Ginny helped in staining and varnishing every piece of wood in the house, it was evident something was wrong.

Having been diagnosed in 1975, her symptoms progressed with Roger assuming near total care by 1983, dressing, feeding, bathing, and toileting his wife. Throughout most of the years of care, Roger assumed full responsibility, wishing to spare his children who he believed had their own lives and responsibilities to manage. As he became progressively depleted in health, endurance, and finances, he appealed for his children's help. In responding, their own lives were adversely affected, and all three were divorced within 6 months. His son, Charles, 45, has since assumed Power of Attorney for his mother.

As his wife's condition deteriorated further, aggravated by frequent seizures and falls, and a weight loss of 40 pounds in a 2-month period, Roger secured the very helpful and loving services of the county visiting nurses for supervised bathing, homemaker services, and so on. Roger's own health had simultaneously declined, and he was hospitalized in July of 1984 for a progressed aneurysm, high blood pressure, and other symptoms, necessitating Ginny's admission to a nursing home. The placement was extremely painful to and long resisted by Roger, who continues to visit Ginny twice daily and who hopes to resume her care at home.

Roger has become an active member and volunteer of the Alzheimer's Disease Association, attending and assisting with support group meetings and appearing on family panels. More recently, he has been involved in plans to lead a husbands' support group.

Particularly traumatic for Roger have been the continued virtual rejection of Ginny by her family of origin and his coming to terms philosophically with her suffering in view of the near sanctity of her life, which was dedicated to bringing children closer to God. Both Roger and his wife have been members of the Zion Lutheran Church, where Roger served as financial secretary for 35 years, and both sang in the choir. Church response has often been disappointing, except for a specially arranged communion service.

STUDENT ACTIVITY

1. Identify the key issues for each member of the family from the perspective of your profession.
2. Identify the barriers your profession would face in attempting to deal effectively with this case.
3. Develop a collaborative model of care for Ginny and her family.

FOR FURTHER DISCUSSION AND STUDY

1. How could an interprofessional approach to this case help minimize or neutralize the constraints and barriers to effective care that you identified in the second activity?
2. What community resources are available to Ginny and her family to assist with her care and their respite?
3. Are professionals obligated to provide care for their clients?

CHAPTER 11

Professional Ethics in the Interprofessional Context
Selected Codes of Professional Ethics

R. Michael Casto, Ph.D.

Codes of professional ethics are generated by professional societies and bodies on behalf of their members. These codes establish standards of behavior and practice in order to protect both professionals and their clients and to safeguard the integrity of the professions.

We have included the codes of selected professions here, and presented some of the activities in Chapter 10, in order to engage you in the discussion and analysis of issues related to personal, professional, and interprofessional ethical decision-making and behavior.

We have also included a suggested oath of commitment for members of an interdisciplinary health care team. The oath illustrates what could or should be included in an interprofessional code of ethics. The oath may also be used as a basis for comparing and contrasting ideal interprofessional requirements and the content of the various professional codes.

Included for discussion are codes of ethics from education, medicine, physical therapy, social work, and theology.

Oath of Commitment for Members of an Interdisciplinary Health Care Team

I promise to fulfill the obligations I voluntarily assume by professing to heal, and to help those who are ill. My obligations rest in the special vulnerability of the sick and the trust they must place in me and my professional competence. I, therefore, bind myself to the good of my patient in its many dimensions as the first principle of my professional ethics. In recognition of this bond, I accept the following obligations from which only the patient or his or her valid surrogate can release me:

A. Duties Toward Patients
1. I will place the good of the patient at the center of my professional practice. Patients will be explicitly informed about what conduct they may expect from me as part of this commitment.
2. When the gravity of the situation demands it, I will place the best interests of the patient over my own self-interest, even over my own life. Thus, I promise to act primarily in behalf of my patient's best interests, and not primarily to advance social, political, or fiscal policy, or my own interests.
3. I promise to respect my patient's moral right to participate in the decisions that affect him or her by explaining, clearly, fairly, and in language understood by the patient, the nature of his or her illness or accident, together with the benefits and burdens of the treatments and interventions I propose, and by respecting the decisions they make about these options.
4. I promise to assist my patients to make choices that coincide with their own values or beliefs, without coercion, deception, or duplicity. In case the patient is incompetent, I will assist validly designated surrogates, or lacking such, the family, in making such choices based on the patient's explicit, presumed, or constructed values.
5. I will care for all persons who need my help with equal concern and dedication, independent of their ability to pay.[1]
6. I will hold in confidence what I hear, learn, and see as a necessary part of my care of the patient, except when there is a clear, serious, and immediate danger of harm to others.
7. I will always help, even when I cannot participate in a cure, and when death is inevitable I will assist the patient to die according to his or her own life plans.
8. Nonetheless, because of my duty to preserve life, I will never participate in direct, active euthanasia, or conscious killing of the patient, even

D. C. Thomasma (1987), reprinted with permission from M. L. Brunner and R. M. Casto (Eds.), *Interdisciplinary health team care: Proceedings of the Eighth Annual Conference.* (Columbus: School of Allied Medical Professions and The Commission on Interprofessional Education and Practice, The Ohio State University), pp. 11–12.

[1] E. D. Pellegrino and D. C. Thomasma (1981), *A philosophical basis of medical practice.* (New York: Oxford University Press), pp. 170–191.

for reasons of mercy, at the request of the state, or for any other reason.[2]

B. Duties to Self
1. I will possess and maintain the competence in knowledge and skill I profess to have.
2. I will acknowledge my own professional and personal limitations to patients, and seek help from other professionals whenever I can for the patient's good.
3. When patients' values or wishes pose a violation of my own conscience, I will make this respectfully known to them, and withdraw from the relationship as soon as another professional can replace me.
4. If I am paid by a health care delivery plan to assist in the control of health care costs, I will reveal this to the patient as a form of self-interest.

C. Duties to Institutions
1. I will assist the development of "committed institutions," that is, the development of institutional health policies based on this code of ethics and other ethical principles that may strengthen the care of patients.
2. I will take constant care to balance the duties to patients with the needs of the institution in which I practice to survive. Nonetheless, the first of my duties remains to the patient.
3. I will reveal to the patient the potential clashes with the institution's moral commitments as soon as possible in the treatment plan, and help arrange for a transfer of the patient should the latter find these commitments intolerable.

D. Duties to Other Health Care Professionals
1. Recognizing the limitations of my own competence, I will call upon colleagues in all the health professions whenever the patient's needs require.
2. I will respect the values and beliefs of my colleagues in any other health profession and recognize their moral accountability as individuals.
3. I will do my best to create interprofessional bonds of respect and deference whenever possible. Thus, I will try to the best of my ability to practice, embody, and teach the values of this code of ethics.

E. Duties to Society
1. To partially fulfill my social obligations, I will participate actively in public policy decisions affecting the nation's health by providing leadership, as well as expert and objective testimony when required.
2. In all efforts to deliver health care, I will remain committed to the primacy of the value of quality of care.

---

[2] Most often, professionals who believe that active euthanasia is sometimes justified base this justification on a promise a professional might make to a patient that the professional would not abandon the patient in his or her suffering. I hold that it is proper for health professionals to administer enough narcotics to control pain and suffering, including psychological suffering, even if such administration may cause death (for example, through insufficient respiratory function induced by the drugs). Cf. E. Cassell. (March 1983). The relief of suffering. *Archives of Internal Medicine, 143,* 522–523.

CODE OF ETHICS OF THE EDUCATION PROFESSION, ADOPTED BY THE 1975 NEA REPRESENTATIVE ASSEMBLY

■ *Preamble*

The educator, believing in the worth and dignity of each human being, recognizes the supreme importance of the pursuit of truth, devotion to excellence, and the nurture of democratic principles. Essential to these goals is the protection of freedom to learn and to teach and the guarantee of equal educational opportunity for all. The educator accepts the responsibility to adhere to the highest ethical standards.

The educator recognizes the magnitude of the responsibility inherent in the teaching process. The desire for the respect and confidence of one's colleagues, of students, of parents, and of the members of the community provides the incentive to attain and maintain the highest possible degree of ethical conduct. The Code of Ethics of the Education Profession indicates the aspiration of all educators and provides standards by which to judge conduct.

The remedies specified by the NEA and/or its affiliates for the violation of any provision of this Code shall be exclusive and no such provision shall be enforceable in any form other than one specifically designated by the NEA or its affiliates.

■ *Principle I—Commitment to the Student*

The educator strives to help each student realize his or her potential as a worthy and effective member of society. The educator therefore works to stimulate the spirit of inquiry, the acquisition of knowledge and understanding, and the thoughtful formulation of worthy goals.

In fulfillment of the obligation to the student, the educator—

1. Shall not unreasonably restrain the student from independent action in the pursuit of learning.
2. Shall not unreasonably deny the student access to varying points of view.
3. Shall not deliberately suppress or distort subject matter relevant to the student's progress.
4. Shall make reasonable effort to protect the student from conditions harmful to learning or to health and safety.
5. Shall not intentionally expose the student to embarrassment or disparagement.
6. Shall not on the basis of race, color, creed, sex, national origin, marital status, political or religious beliefs, family, social or cultural background, or sexual orientation, unfairly:

a. Exclude any student from participation in any program;
b. Deny benefits to any student;
c. Grant any advantage to any student.
7. Shall not use professional relationships with students for private advantage.
8. Shall not disclose information about students obtained in the course of professional service unless disclosure serves a compelling professional purpose or is required by law.

■ *Principle II—Commitment to the Profession*

The education profession is vested by the public with a trust and responsibility requiring the highest ideals of professional service.

In the belief that the quality of the services of the education profession directly influences the nation and its citizens, the educator shall exert every effort to raise professional standards, to promote a climate that encourages the exercise of professional judgment, to achieve conditions that attract persons worthy of the trust to careers in education, and to assist in preventing the practice of the profession by unqualified persons.

In fulfillment of the obligation to the profession, the educator—

1. Shall not in an application for a professional position deliberately make a false statement or fail to disclose a material fact related to competency and qualifications.
2. Shall not misrepresent his/her professional qualifications.
3. Shall not assist entry into the profession of a person known to be unqualified in respect to character, education, or other relevant attribute.
4. Shall not knowingly make a false statement concerning the qualifications of a candidate for a professional position.
5. Shall not assist a noneducator in the unauthorized practice of teaching.
6. Shall not disclose information about colleagues obtained in the course of professional service unless disclosure serve a compelling professional purpose or is required by law.
7. Shall not knowingly make false or malicious statements about a colleague.
8. Shall not accept any gratuity, gift, or favor that might impair or appear to influence professional decisions or actions.

THE HIPPOCRATIC OATH

I swear by Apollo the healer, invoking all the gods and goddesses to be my witnesses, that I will fulfil this Oath and this written Covenant to the best of my ability and judgment.

Adapted with permission: American Medical Association, 1993.

I will look upon him who shall have taught me this Art even as one of my own parents. I will share my substance with him, and I will supply his necessities, if he be in need. I will regard his offspring even as my own brethren, and I will teach them this Art, if they would learn it, without fee or covenant. I will impart this Art by precept, by lecture and by every mode of teaching, not only to my own sons but to the sons of him who taught me, and to disciples bound by covenant and oath, according to the Law of Medicine.

The regimen I adopt shall be for the benefit of the patients according to my ability and judgment, and not for their hurt or for any wrong. I will give no deadly drug to any, though it be asked of me, nor will I counsel such, and especially I will not aid a woman to procure abortion. Whatsoever house I enter, there will I go for the benefit of the sick, refraining from all wrongdoing or corruption, and especially from any act of seduction, of male or female, of bond or free. Whatsoever things I see or hear concerning the life of men, in my attendance on the sick or even apart therefrom, which ought not to be noised abroad, I will keep silence thereon, counting such things to be sacred secrets. Pure and holy will I keep my Life and my Art.

If I fulfil this Oath and confound it not, be it mine to enjoy Life and Art alike, with good repute among all men at all times. If I transgress and violate my oath, may the reverse be my lot.

AMERICAN MEDICAL ASSOCIATION PRINCIPLES OF MEDICAL ETHICS

■ *Preamble*

The medical profession has long subscribed to a body of ethical statements developed primarily for the benefit of the patient. As a member of this profession, a physician must recognize responsibility not only to patients, but also to society, to other health professionals, and to self. The following Principles adopted by the American Medical Association are not laws, but standards of conduct which define the essentials of honorable behavior for the physician.

   I. A physician shall be dedicated to providing competent medical service with compassion and respect for human dignity.
  II. A physician shall deal honestly with patients and colleagues, and strive to expose those physicians deficient in character or competence, or who engage in fraud or deception.
 III. A physician shall respect the law and also recognize a responsibility to seek changes in those requirements which are contrary to the best interests of the patient.

IV. A physician shall respect the rights of patients, of colleagues, and of other health professionals, and shall safeguard patient confidences within the constraints of the law.

V. A physician shall continue to study, apply, and advance scientific knowledge, make relevant information available to patients, colleagues, and the public, obtain consultation, and use the talents of other health professionals when indicated.

VI. A physician shall, in the provision of appropriate patient care, except in emergencies, be free to choose whom to serve, with whom to associate, and the environment in which to provide medical services.

VII. A physician shall recognize a responsibility to participate in activities contributing to an improved community.

AMERICAN PHYSICAL THERAPY ASSOCIATION CODE OF ETHICS

■ *Preamble*

This Code of Ethics sets forth ethical principles for the physical therapy profession. Members of this profession are responsible for maintaining and promoting ethical practice. This Code of Ethics, adopted by the American Physical Therapy Association, shall be binding on physical therapists who are members of the Association.

■ *Principle 1*

Physical therapists respect the rights and dignity of all individuals.

■ *Principle 2*

Physical therapists comply with the laws and regulations governing the practice of physical therapy.

■ *Principle 3*

Physical therapists accept responsibility for the exercise of sound judgment.

■ *Principle 4*

Physical therapists maintain and promote high standards in the provision of physical therapy services.

■ *Principle 5*

Physical therapists seek remuneration for their services that is deserved and reasonable.

■ *Principle 6*

Physical therapists provide accurate information to the consumer about the profession and about those services they provide.

■ *Principle 7*

Physical therapists accept the responsibility to protect the public and the profession from unethical, incompetent, or illegal acts.

■ *Principle 8*

Physical therapists participate in efforts to address the health needs of the public.

THE NATIONAL ASSOCIATION OF SOCIAL WORKERS CODE OF ETHICS

I. The Social Worker's Conduct and Comportment as a Social Worker
   A. Propriety—The social worker should maintain high standards of personal conduct in the capacity or identity as social worker.
      1. The private conduct of the social worker is a personal matter to the same degree as is any other person's, except when such conduct compromises the fulfillment of professional responsibilities.
      2. The social worker should not participate in, condone, or be associated with dishonesty, fraud, deceit, or misrepresentation.
      3. The social worker should distinguish clearly between statements and actions made as a private individual and as a representative of the social work profession or an organization or group.

B. Competence and Professional Development—The social worker should strive to become and remain proficient in professional practice and the performance of professional functions.
   1. The social worker should accept responsibility or employment only on the basis of existing competence or the intention to acquire the necessary competence.
   2. The social worker should not misrepresent professional qualifications, education, experience, or affiliations.
C. Service—The social worker should regard as primary the service obligation of the social work profession.
   1. The social worker should retain ultimate responsibility for the quality and extent of the service that individual assumes, assigns, or performs.
   2. The social worker should act to prevent practices that are inhumane or discriminatory against any person or group of persons.
D. Integrity—The social worker should act in accordance with the highest standards of professional integrity and impartiality.
   1. The social worker should be alert to and resist the influences and pressures that interfere with the exercise of professional discretion and impartial judgment required for the performance of professional functions.
   2. The social worker should not exploit professional relationships for personal gain.
E. Scholarship and Research—The social worker engaged in study and research should be guided by the conventions of scholarly inquiry.
   1. The social worker engaged in research should consider carefully its possible consequences for human beings.
   2. The social worker engaged in research should ascertain that the consent of participants in the research is voluntary and informed, without any implied deprivation or penalty for refusal to participate, and with due regard for participants' privacy and dignity.
   3. The social worker engaged in research should protect participants from unwarranted physical or mental discomfort, distress, harm, danger, or deprivation.
   4. The social worker who engages in the evaluation of services or cases should discuss them only for the professional purposes and only with people directly and professionally concerned with them.
   5. Information obtained about participants in research should be treated as confidential.
   6. The social worker should take credit only for work actually done in connection with scholarly and research endeavors and credit contributions made by others.
II. The Social Worker's Ethical Responsibility to Clients
   F. Primacy of Client's Interests—The social worker's primary responsibility is to clients.
      1. The social worker should serve clients with devotion, loyalty, de-

       termination, and the maximum application of professional skill and competence.

2. The social worker should not exploit relationships with clients for personal advantage, or solicit the clients of one's agency for private practice.

3. The social worker should not practice, condone, facilitate, or collaborate with any form of discrimination on the basis of race, color, sex, sexual orientation, age, religion, national origin, marital status, political belief, mental or physical handicap, or any other preference or personal characteristic, condition, or status.

4. The social worker should avoid relationships or commitments that conflict with the interests of the client.

5. The social worker should under no circumstances engage in sexual activities with clients.

6. The social worker should provide clients with accurate and complete information regarding the extent and nature of the services available to them.

7. The social worker should apprise clients of their risks, rights, opportunities, and obligations associated with social service to them.

8. The social worker should seek advice and counsel of colleagues and supervisors whenever such consultation is in the best interest of clients.

9. The social worker should terminate service to clients, and professional relationships with them, when such service and relationships are no longer required or no longer serve the clients' needs or interests.

10. The social worker should withdraw services precipitously only under unusual circumstances, giving careful consideration to all factors in the situation and taking care to minimize possible adverse effects.

11. The social worker who anticipates the termination or interruption of service to clients should notify clients promptly and seek the transfer, referral, or continuation of service in relation to the clients' needs and preferences.

G. Rights and Prerogatives of Clients—The social worker should make every effort to foster maximum self-determination on the part of clients.

1. When the social worker must act on behalf of a client who has been adjudged legally incompetent, the social worker should safeguard the interests and rights of that client.

2. When another individual has been legally authorized to act in behalf of a client, the social worker should deal with that person always with the client's best interest in mind.

3. The social worker should not engage in any action that violates or diminishes the civil or legal rights of clients.

H. Confidentiality and Privacy—The social worker should respect the privacy of clients and hold in confidence all information obtained in the course of professional service.

1. The social worker should share with others confidences revealed by clients, without their consent, only for compelling professional reasons.
2. The social worker should inform clients fully about the limits of confidentiality in a given situation, the purposes for which information is obtained, and how it may be used.
3. The social worker should afford clients reasonable access to any official social work records concerning them.
4. When providing clients with access to records, the social worker should take due care to protect the confidences of others contained in those records.
5. The social worker should obtain informed consent of clients before taping, recording, or permitting third party observation of their activities.

I. Fees—When setting fees, the social worker should ensure that they are fair, reasonable, considerate, and commensurate with the service performed and with due regard for the clients' ability to pay.

1. The social worker should not divide a fee or accept or give anything of value for receiving or making a referral.

III. The Social Worker's Ethical Responsibility to Colleagues

J. Respect, Fairness, and Courtesy—The social worker should treat colleagues with respect, courtesy, fairness, and good faith.

1. The social worker should cooperate with colleagues to promote professional interests and concerns.
2. The social worker should respect confidences shared by colleagues in the course of their professional relationships and transactions.
3. The social worker should create and maintain conditions of practice that facilitate ethical and competent professional performance by colleagues.
4. The social worker should treat with respect, and represent accurately and fairly, the qualifications, views, and findings of colleagues and use appropriate channels to express judgments on these matters.
5. The social worker who replaces or is replaced by a colleague in professional practice should act with consideration for the interest, character, and reputation of that colleague.
6. The social worker should not exploit a dispute between a colleague and employers to obtain a position or otherwise advance the social worker's interest.
7. The social worker should seek arbitration or mediation when conflicts with colleagues require resolution for compelling professional reasons.
8. The social worker should extend to colleagues of other professions

the same respect and cooperation that is extended to social work colleagues.

   9. The social worker who serves as an employer, supervisor, or mentor to colleagues should make orderly and explicit arrangements regarding the conditions of their continuing professional relationship.

  10. The social worker who has the responsibility for employing and evaluating the performance of other staff members should fulfill such responsibility in a fair, considerate, and equitable manner, on the basis of clearly enunciated criteria.

  11. The social worker who has responsibility for evaluating the performance of employees, supervisors, or students should share evaluations with them.

K. Dealing with Colleagues' Clients—The social worker has the responsibility to relate to the clients of colleagues with full professional consideration.

  1. The social worker should not solicit the clients of colleagues.

  2. The social worker should not assume professional responsibility for the clients of another agency or a colleague without appropriate communication with that agency or colleague.

  3. The social worker who serves the clients of colleagues, during a temporary absence or emergency, should serve those clients with the same consideration as that afforded any client.

IV. The Social Worker's Ethical Responsibility to Employers and Employing Organizations

L. Commitments to Employing Organization—The social worker should adhere to commitments made to the employing organization.

  1. The social worker should work to improve the employing agency's policies and procedures, and the efficiency and effectiveness of its services.

  2. The social worker should not accept employment or arrange student field placements in an organization which is currently under public sanction by NASW for violating personnel standards, or imposing limitations on or penalties for professional actions on behalf of clients.

  3. The social worker should act to prevent and eliminate discrimination in the employing organization's work assignments and in its employment policies and practices.

  4. The social worker should use with scrupulous regard, and only for the purpose for which they are intended, the resources of the employing organization.

V. The Social Worker's Ethical Responsibility to the Social Work Profession

M. Maintaining the Integrity of the Profession—The social worker should uphold and advance the values, ethics, knowledge, and mission of the profession.

1. The social worker should protect and enhance the dignity and integrity of the profession and should be responsible and vigorous in discussion and criticism of the profession.
2. The social worker should take action through appropriate channels against unethical conduct by any other member of the profession.
3. The social worker should act to prevent the unauthorized and unqualified practice of social work.
4. The social worker should make no misrepresentation in advertising as to qualifications, competence, service, or results to be achieved.

N. Community Service—The social worker should assist the profession in making social services available to the general public.
1. The social worker should contribute time and professional expertise to activities that promote respect for the utility, the integrity, and the competence of the social work profession.
2. The social worker should support the formulation, development, enactment and implementation of social policies of concern to the profession.

O. Development of Knowledge—The social worker should take responsibility for identifying, developing, and fully utilizing knowledge for professional practice.
1. The social worker should base practice upon recognized knowledge relevant to social work.
2. The social worker should critically examine and keep current with emerging knowledge relevant to social work.

VI. The Social Worker's Ethical Responsibility to Society
P. Promoting the General Welfare—The social worker should promote the general welfare of society.
1. The social worker should act to prevent and eliminate discrimination against any person or group on the basis of race, color, sex, sexual orientation, age, religion, national origin, marital status, political belief, mental or physical handicap, or any other preference or personal characteristic, condition, or status.
2. The social worker should act to ensure that all persons have access to the resources, services, and opportunities which they require.
3. The social worker should act to expand choice and opportunity for all persons, with special regard for disadvantaged or oppressed groups and persons.
4. The social worker should promote conditions that encourage respect for the diversity of cultures which constitute American society.
5. The social worker should provide appropriate professional services in public emergencies.
6. The social worker should advocate changes in policy and legislation to improve social conditions and to promote social justice.
7. The social worker should encourage informed participation by the public in shaping social policies and institutions.

Evangelical Lutheran Church in America: Definitions and Guidelines for Discipline of Ordained Ministers

As an expression of its life in the gospel of Jesus Christ, this church embraces disciplinary processes of counseling, admonition, and correction, with the objective of forgiveness, reconciliation, and healing.

Simultaneously, out of deep concern for effective extension of the gospel, this church remains alert to the high calling of discipleship in Jesus Christ. The ordained ministers of this church, as persons charged with special responsibility for the proclamation of the gospel, are to seek to reflect the new life in Christ, avoiding that which would make them stumbling blocks to others. To that end, this church recognizes that there is behavior that is deemed to be incompatible with the ordained ministry, and that calls for disciplinary action.

The following definitions and guidelines do not set forth the high expectations this church has of its ordained ministers. (A document of such expectations has been developed by the Division for Ministry for this church.) The normative expectations of this church for its ordained ministers focus upon faithful and effective exercise of ministerial leadership. In all matters of morality and personal ethics, this church expects its ordained ministers to be exemplary in conduct.

These definitions and guidelines describe the grounds for which ordained ministers may be subject to discipline according to the practice of this church. Their purpose is juridical: to assist in the processes of consultation, discipline, and appeals.

Grounds for discipline of ordained ministers are as follows:

A. Preaching or teaching in conflict with the faith confessed by this church is grounds for discipline of ordained ministers. A summary of the faith confessed by this church is found in Chapters 2 and 3 of this church's constitution.

B. Conduct incompatible with the character of the ministerial office is grounds for discipline of ordained ministers. These guidelines define and describe kinds of behavior which are incompatible with the character of the ministerial office.

1. Confidential Communications

   Ordained ministers must respect privileged and confidential communication and may not disclose such communication, except with the express permission of the person who has confided it or if the person is perceived to intend great harm to self or others.

2. Professional Attention to Duties

   An ordained minister of this church has made commitments through ordination and through acceptance of a letter of call. Continued neglect of or indifference toward such duties constitutes conduct incompatible with the character of the ministerial office.

Approved by the Church Council, Evangelical Lutheran Church in America, November 1989.

3. Relationship to Family

   This church is committed to the sanctity of marriage and the enhance-
   ment of family life. Ordained ministers of this church, whether married
   or single, are expected to uphold Christian ideals of marriage in their
   public ministry as well as in private life. Spouse and children, if any, are
   to be regarded with love, respect and commitment.

   Any departure from this normative behavior may be considered conduct incompatible with the character of the ministerial office. Such
   departure might include any of the following:

   a. Separation or divorce that occurs without consultation with the
      synodical bishop's office and appropriate implementation of such
      consultation. Each relationship must be considered pastorally.
   b. Desertion or abandonment of spouse or children.
   c. Abuse of spouse or children.
   d. Repeated failure to meet legally determined family support obliga-
      tions.

4. Sexual Matters

   The biblical understanding which this church affirms is that the normative setting for sexual intercourse is marriage. In keeping with this
   understanding, chastity before marriage and fidelity within marriage is
   the norm. Adultery, promiscuity, the sexual abuse of another, or the
   misuse of counseling relationships for sexual favors constitute conduct
   that is incompatible with the character of the ministerial office. Practicing homosexual persons are precluded from the ordained ministry of
   this church.

5. Substance Abuse

   Misuse of alcohol or mind-altering substances impairs the ability of an
   ordained minister to perform the duties of the office with full effectiveness. The approach of this church in dealing with such a problem is to
   recommend and enable effective treatment. However, failure to accept
   treatment or to follow through on treatment and abide by the terms of
   such treatment and the consequent impairment of performance is
   conduct incompatible with the character of the ministerial office.

6. Fiscal Responsibilities

   Ordained ministers of this church are expected to conduct their fiscal
   affairs in accordance with ethical and legal requirements. Among those
   fiscal activities that may be considered conduct incompatible with the
   character of the ministerial office are:

   a. Indifference to or avoidance of legitimate and neglected personal
      debts.
   b. Embezzlement of money or improper appropriation of the property
      of others.
   c. Using the ministerial office improperly for personal financial advan-
      tage.

7. Membership in Certain Organizations

   This church has specifically declared in 7.47.01 that discipline may be administered to any of its ordained ministers who belongs to any organization other than the church which claims to possess in its teaching and ceremonies that which the Lord has given solely to the Church.

8. Conviction of a Felony

The society in which this church ministers has placed a high premium upon the role of law in regulating the rights and duties of individuals to promote the common good. This includes laws which define certain conduct as felonies. Pleading guilty to, or being convicted of, a felony is grounds for discipline as conduct incompatible with the character of the ministerial office, but may not be grounds for discipline in those instances where the violation of law was to protest or to test a perceived unjust law or as an expression of civil disobedience.

C. Willfully disregarding or violating the functions and standards established by this church for the office of Word and sacrament is grounds for discipline of ordained ministers. Such functions and standards established by this church are found in Section 7.20 through 7.47.01 of this church's constitution, bylaws and continuing resolutions.

D. Willful disregard of the constitution or bylaws of this church is grounds for discipline of ordained ministers. However, the disciplinary sanction of removal from the ordained ministry is limited by 20.21.02.

PART 5

Reflections

CHAPTER 12

Program Model for Interprofessional Education
A Case Study

R. Michael Casto, M.Div., Ph.D.

An important question for those who educate professionals focuses on the transition from theoretical assumptions about interprofessional education to the reality of teaching interprofessional collaboration in the context of professional education programs. One model for such an educational program is the Commission on Interprofessional Education and Practice at The Ohio State University. Its program and curricula are based on the principles outlined in this book.

HISTORY AND STRUCTURE

The Commission on Interprofessional Education and Practice at The Ohio State University brings together members of the human service professions (allied medicine, education, law, medicine, nursing, psychology, social work, and theology) to address collaboratively the complex ethical and social problems increasingly encountered in professional practice. The commission was founded in 1973 with funding from the Ohio Board of Regents to provide both pre-professional and continuing education.

The commission is supported by its constituent members, each of which has a seat on its board of directors: The Ohio State University colleges of education, law, medicine, nursing, social work, school of allied medical professions and office of academic affairs; the Columbus Cluster of Theological Schools, comprising Methodist Theological School in Ohio, Pontifical College Josephinum, and Trinity Lutheran Seminary; and state-level professional associations including the Ohio Chapter of the National Association of Social Workers, the Ohio Council of Churches, the Ohio Nurses Association, the Ohio Psychological Association, the Ohio Society of Allied Health Professions, the Ohio State Bar Association, the Ohio State Medical Association, and the Ohio Education Association. It has also received support for specific projects from various federal agencies and foundations, including the W. K. Kellogg Foundation and the Columbus Foundation.

Van Bogard Dunn, then dean of the Methodist Theological School in Ohio, became the first chairman of the commission in 1973 and guided it throughout its developing years. Luvern L. Cunningham, then Novice G. Fawcett professor of educational administration, OSU College of Education, became chairperson on July 1, 1980. A Committee of Deans of the participating colleges serves as a supervisory body for the commission with special concern for curriculum and the quality of the credit education offerings. The Committee of Deans also functions as a link between the commission and the OSU Office of Academic Affairs.

GOALS AND OBJECTIVES

The goals of the commission are threefold: (1) to provide interprofessional education for students of selected human service professions; (2) to provide continuing education courses, conferences, and assemblies for practicing professionals from those disciplines; and (3) to facilitate interprofessional panels for the analysis and formulation of public policy.

The four educational objectives of the commission are

1. to address interprofessionally a range of ethical issues arising out of technological change
2. to identify changing societal values and prepare professional students for their role in responding to and shaping them
3. to teach concepts and methods of interprofessional teamwork in treating the interrelated problems of the whole person at the case level
4. to improve the human condition through interprofessional analysis of public policy issues

■ *Case Study Methodology*

Each of the courses employs a case study methodology to achieve its goals and objectives. Cases are developed by faculty teaching in the course. They draw on their professional experience, cases used in prior years, and cases generated by faculty and students in their own practice. Cases are submitted to the entire faculty for revision and review. An attempt is made to be as comprehensive as possible by including each of the professions that participate in the course. However, this comprehensiveness is not achieved by sacrificing realism and authenticity. The effectiveness of cases is measured in relation to achieving the goals of the course. (See Chapter 10 for sample cases.)

Since most of the professions included in the interprofessional curriculum commonly use the case study method, students are usually already familiar with its potential for illustrating professional practice problems. However, they may not be aware of the dimensions of collaborative practice explored in the interprofessional courses. Since most cases have their origin in practice settings, students are able to evaluate circumstances realistically in relation to presented data.

Occasionally students desire more information than is included in any particular case presentation, especially when questions of ethical issues and social values are being considered. Such requests tend to focus attention on the case and away from the specific ethical issue or value question. Most students are able to understand this distinction once they are made aware of it.

Cases are designed to illustrate the particular problems under consideration and to give the group the opportunity to work together in analyzing problems, proposing solutions, and developing treatment plans. In using the case study method, the faculties hope to focus attention on the interprofessional process and enable students to develop skills in interprofessional collaboration. Solutions to particular cases are only incidental to that educational aim. The case study method is used so that students can experience the strength of the interprofessional collaborative process.

Faculty are aware of the philosophical debate concerning the validity of the case study approach to teaching (Hewitt, 1983). Students are not expected to generalize from their experience with specific cases to the remainder of their practice, especially in relation to particular client problems. Rather, the focus is on the interprofessional process. It would seem, therefore, that the use of a case study method is a justified pedagogical tool in teaching effective interprofessional collaboration. Indeed, faculty and students have consistently suggested that the use of cases helps students ground their course experience in the realities of professional practice. This method enables them to avoid abstractions and generalizations. Students are required to test their collaborative skills in relation to the kinds of complex problems they will encounter in actual practice. Further, since the focus of the learning objective is on the process itself rather than the particular problems and issues of the case, students are enabled to formulate an understanding of the nature of that process in terms that are meaningful to their particular professional skills and self-understandings.

■ *Academic Coordination*

The academic portion of the program requires coordination and attention to the details necessary to bring together diverse departments within the university. An academic coordinator provides continuity from one faculty team to another, both within a given course and between different courses. The coordinator also provides administrative support for the faculty teams, coordinates their meetings, arranges facilities, oversees and coordinates the work of research projects related to the academic program, acts as a liaison between the academic units, and assists in publicizing courses and recruiting students. The coordinator also provides resources for the faculty team and faculty development opportunities.

The coordinating function is both a sign of the institution's commitment to providing an ongoing program and a necessary element in the administration of a program of education for interprofessional practice. Most universities are organized vertically. Dollars and decisions are negotiated independently within colleges, departments, or divisions. Each academic unit evolves its own administrative structure and style and its own internal political dynamic. Attempts to cooperate with other academic units usually run against the grain of the established structures.

The academic coordinator must operate horizontally in this vertical world, acting as a bridge from one academic unit to another. The coordinator must maintain close working relationships with each academic unit at all levels, administrative, faculty, and clerical. Maintaining those relationships requires sensitivity to the internal dynamics of each unit and its particular administrative organization and style.

The academic coordinator must have a clear conception of the total program of education for interprofessional practice and a vision of its goals. The coordinator must also understand the program's value for both students and faculty. That value must be achieved for the participants through the careful selection of faculty, nurturance of the faculty teaching team, development of course syllabi and resources, and attention to the details of activities throughout every course. In this sense, the academic coordinator is an advocate for the academic program and its faculty.

The academic coordinator provides learning experiences for the faculty as well as the occasion for them to develop their own interprofessional skills. The coordinator must be attentive to the details of team dynamics within the faculty team and assist the team in its efforts to develop as a teaching team. The coordinator also has the opportunity to provide resources developed in other faculty teams and to guard against overlapping subject matter between courses.

While the heart of a program in education for interprofessional practice remains the faculty team, the tasks and functions of academic coordination are a necessary ingredient in facilitating that program. Whether these functions are located in a single individual or distributed between team members, they need to be accomplished in order for the team to carry out its teaching task. An institution anticipating establishing a program of education for interprofessional practice will need to seriously consider and provide for this coordinating function.

■ Class Activities and Groupings

The interprofessional courses employ several common teaching methodologies and activities. In each course, theoretical and conceptual material as well as cases are presented in plenary sessions. Conceptual lectures are generally followed by a case presentation or a discussion that includes the remaining faculty members and students.

Following the plenary introductions of topics, students gather in professional groups. At this time, the professional faculty member leads the students in a discussion to identify relevant issues from the perspective of their profession. Such issue identification may result in assignments for research and exploration in preparation for the next phase of the process, the interprofessional discussion.

By approaching the issue or case from the perspective of one's own profession prior to engaging in an interprofessional discussion, students are encouraged to give consideration to the topic using the expertise of their profession. Such an approach encourages the student to be the most productive and well-equipped professional that he or she can be before engaging in the interprofessional discussion. An important conviction of faculty and others involved in the planning process is the principle that interprofessional collaboration should not become a substitute for professional competence. Students should approach interprofessional discussion as skilled professionals.

The interprofessional discussion group is the heart of each of the courses. The group provides the opportunity for the students to experience the collaborative process in relation to the specific issues and cases presented in the class. It encourages a high degree of interchange among students from various professions and allows students to experience firsthand the strength of the interprofessional approach to complex problems. The goals for the interprofessional discussion may vary depending on the particular subject matter of the course. In courses focusing on interprofessional care, the interprofessional group session is designed to explore the issues that have been identified in professional groups. The group identifies collaborative solutions to those issues. Finally, the students in these courses are engaged in the development of a collaborative care plan that could be implemented in relation to the specific case.

In courses focusing on ethical issues or values, the students in the interprofessional group are encouraged to further explore the ideas and concepts that have emerged in their professional groups. The goal of these discussions is to refine and deepen understanding of the issues by means of interprofessional collaboration.

Student evaluations consistently indicate that the interprofessional dimensions of the courses are a high point in their educational careers. Indeed, most students argue for more time in interprofessional groups and less time in plenary sessions and professional group discussions. Students value the opportunity to exchange their ideas and expertise with those from other professions, as well as the opportunity to gain insights into the perspectives of the other professions. Most students indicate that the interprofessional courses provide the first opportunity they have had in their professional education for such discussion. They argue persuasively that this opportunity allows them to gain new perspectives on cases, to provide better care for their clients, and to develop a broader perspective on the issues they confront in their professional practice. These perceptions are confirmed by both practicing professionals and graduate students.

Interprofessional collaboration is at the heart of the learning that takes place in the courses. Professional barriers are dissolved, and turf issues become less important. Perhaps most important, issues are explored more fully, and clients are provided with better care.

Finally, to conclude and summarize the learnings from each topic following the interprofessional group meetings, students gather once again in plenary session. At this time they discuss with faculty and other students the points made, the issues raised, and the treatments proposed in their interprofessional group sessions.

This plenary session also provides an opportunity for the students to experience the faculty as an interprofessional team. Faculty panels also provide such an opportunity. More frequently, informal faculty discussions provide an opportunity to explore the issues and cases in even greater depth, to identify learnings, and to promote dialogue between the faculty and students. Faculty and students have an opportunity to explore the interprofessional process, and students have a chance to share their observations about group process.

In certain of the courses, opportunities are provided for clinical or field experience with actual clients in settings where interprofessional collaboration is occurring. These are important opportunities for students to observe teams in practice. Clinical experience presents a realistic view of teams collaborating to address complex issues and cases. Further, field experience provides the opportunity for students to apply to actual cases the skills they have learned.

Students are encouraged in some of the courses to establish their own field experience placement or to assemble their own interprofessional team. This experience provides a further opportunity for learning. The students are required to draw on their own resources to establish a team. They experience both the difficulties and the rewards of this process.

In participating in clinical experiences and in establishing their own opportunities for field experience, students may be engaging in the most appropriate and significant learning possible. The knowledge they acquire is based on actual experience with cases and issues in settings where care is in fact being delivered. Such learning may have the most potential to affect the future practice of students.

■ *Educational Outcomes*

Student and faculty evaluations have consistently pointed toward certain elements as being valuable in all of the courses. Among these is interprofessional interaction. Both groups agree that interaction is at the heart of interprofessional collaboration. Participants identify the opportunity for such interaction as the highlight of the courses. More specifically, students consider as significant experiences in the courses the opportunities to learn about other professions; to meet individual professionals; to exchange ideas, perceptions, and feelings; and to address complex social issues or complex client problems.

Further studies conducted by the commission have indicated some significant shifts in attitudes among students (Casto et al., 1985, 1986). Findings indicate that students develop a more positive attitude toward the other professions. Further, they develop a more positive attitude toward the use of conflict in the resolution of complex problems. They see conflict as an important tool to enable discussion, to elucidate ideas, and to further enhance communication. Rather than striving simply for cooperation in groups, they believe that differing opinions and ideas enable the group to arrive at a more comprehensive and complete discussion of the issues or analysis of the cases.

Finally, it is only as interprofessional education impacts the actual practice of students entering the professions that this kind of education has real value and potential for serving the needs of clients. To serve clients better is the ultimate goal of the program of interprofessional education at The Ohio State University. Studies have been conducted asking practicing professionals to assess the impact of interprofessional education on their practice (Spencer, 1983; Harbaugh et al., 1987). These studies demonstrate that professionals who have had courses in interprofessional education consistently identify those courses as having increased the effectiveness of their practice, eased their entry into their practice of their profession, and helped them to provide better care for their clients.

CONCLUSION

The Commission on Interprofessional Education and Practice at The Ohio State University offers a unique program model for exploring a wide range of approaches to collaborative education, practice, policy formulation, and research. In particular, its education program for people preparing to practice in the human service professions offers opportunities for students to explore and practice concepts that will influence their professional self-understanding throughout their careers. The experience of interprofessional collaboration inherent in this model program encourages students to extend the horizon of their own vision to include other professionals as they confront the ethical, value, and care questions that arise in our increasingly complex society. The chief aims of the model program of interprofessional education are to enhance the quality of care provided by the human service professions and to develop a more humane world in which to live and work. Such goals must serve as the motivating force for any program of education for interprofessional practice.

REFERENCES AND RELATED READINGS

Casto, R. M., Nystrom, E. P., and Burgess-Ellison, J. A. (1985). Interprofessional education and attitude change: Research design and the collaborative process. In M. R. Schiller (Ed.), *Collaborative research in allied health* (pp. 51–57). Columbus: The School of Allied Health Professions, The Ohio State University.

Casto, R. M., Nystrom, E. P., and Burgess-Ellison, J. A. (1986). Interprofessional collaboration: Attitude change among students engaged in interprofessional education. In M. J. Lipetz and M. Suvada (Eds.), *Proceedings of the Seventh Annual Conference on Interdisciplinary Health Team Care* (pp. 201–216). Chicago: The Center for Educational Development, The University of Illinois at Chicago.

Harbaugh, G. L., Casto, R. M., and Burgess-Ellison, J. A. (Spring 1987). Becoming a professional: How interprofessional training helps. *Theory into Practice, XXVI* (2), 141–145.

Hewitt, C. M. K. (1983). The ministry case as phenomenon. In D. P. Beisswenger and D. McCarty (Eds.), *Pastoral Theology and Ministry: Key Resources, Vol. IV: Pastoral Hermeneutics and Ministry* (pp. 66–71). Nashville: Association for Theological Field Education.

Spencer, M. H. (1983). *Assessing the impact of interprofessional education on the attitudes and behaviors of practicing professionals.* Unpublished Ph.D. dissertation, The Ohio State University.

CHAPTER 13

A Case Study in Interprofessional Collaboration
The Process of Writing This Book

María C. Juliá, M.S.W., Ph.D.
R. Michael Casto, M.Div., Ph.D.

The Commission on Interprofessional Education and Practice at The Ohio State University began to assist participating academic units by coordinating courses in interprofessional collaboration in 1973. Faculty of these courses believed that the subject matter was essential to effective professional practice. Unfortunately, they soon discovered that resources necessary for optimal teaching and learning were extremely limited. There were no texts written from an interprofessional perspective that addressed the skills necessary for interprofessional collaboration.

The members of the faculty team who participated in shaping and writing this book recognized this deficiency and shared a common perspective. They had all taught in a seminar on the interprofessional care of clients with complex problems. Each of them shared a concern for the availability of materials to teach the knowledge and skills necessary for effective interprofessional collaboration. They all had experienced the difficulty of teaching without effective materials. And, perhaps most significantly, they all had accumulated through their own teaching experience a wealth of knowledge about their subject matter.

Throughout the project the group provided its own leadership. It operated as a consensus group and took full advantage of the opportunity to practice and experience interprofessional collaboration within its own life. The Commission on Interprofessional Education and Practice provided staff support for the project. The staff facilitated the work of the group by caring for its organizational life, providing materials as requested, and offering research assistance.

THE PROCESS OF GROUP WRITING

How to go about developing the book was the central question. Originally, the idea of a multiprofessional collection of contributions was contemplated and favored because of its feasibility in terms of time and resources. The time and energy required to develop an interprofessional product was seen as making the task virtually impossible. The search for direction involved hours of brainstorming and going back and forth between alternative approaches to the work.

With time, the idea of an interprofessional product began to take shape and evolved from the team. The group agreed on a process in which the product would be unique, interprofessional, and as different as possible from the multiprofessional or intraprofessional resources already available.

Although the group was clear about what it wanted to develop, developing the book required extensive discussions about the nature, content, and scope of interprofessional collaboration. The team quickly achieved a shared view of the nature and content of the book. Agreements on scope and particularly processes took longer to achieve. These initial agreements determined the concepts to be discussed, the conceptual outline, and the distribution of initial tasks among team members. Based on individual preferences and strengths, each faculty member agreed to develop one of the themes making up the overall conceptual framework.

Each group member was to review the literature on the concept selected, review the various levels of intervention of the helping professions, apply these to interprofessional collaboration, and include illustrations of the different disciplines. In order to accomplish these tasks, the group held concurrent discussions of the concepts selected as well as of interprofessional collaboration. Through this process the team attempted to guarantee that the language, values, and knowledge of each profession were included in the discussion of concepts as developed by individual authors.

After discussing each concept extensively, team members decided that the team was ready to focus and outline specific elements of the project from the broader perspective of the entire group. Each author's work was followed closely by the group in order to avoid losing the perspectives that the other authors on the team had expressed.

Because of the diverse professional perspectives represented, the discussion of every concept involved frequent digressions about the direction to take.

The concept of interprofessional collaboration was simultaneously redefined and clarified in relation to what it meant to each member of the group. The group carefully discussed how each profession views the client as well as the shared response of caring for clients. All of this discussion greatly influenced the final content of the book.

Following these extensive discussions, and in order to ensure maximum involvement by every group member in the writing of each piece of the work, the team decided that each member would present his or her original set of compiled ideas on the selected concept before the entire group. This presentation was made only after each participant had routed a draft of his or her ideas to all members for their feedback.

All members of the group took the Myers-Briggs Type Indicator test. An extensive discussion of personality types, interactions, and their impact on the process of the group was a necessary component of the development of the book.[1] This discussion helped the group clarify relationships and working styles and achieve more effective working relationships.

After initial feedback on each of the original sets of ideas, the group completed a preliminary draft of all the chapters. The group went on its first two-day retreat, where every piece of work with further revisions was again presented and discussed. This time, although the entire group was still responsible for providing feedback for the entire manuscript, two members other than the primary author or authors were assigned to each chapter for an in-depth review. This process generated more changes to the content of each chapter. The process was repeated again with two different group members serving as reviewers. Every chapter not only received ongoing feedback from the entire group but was reviewed and revised in great detail by at least five members of the group—the original author or authors of the chapter and four reviewers.

Each group member believes that his or her personal and professional growth as a member of this interprofessional team has been unusual and exciting. Looking back, this experience provided a laboratory for interprofessional teamwork, where the contribution of every professional on the team was important to the team goal. Of particular interest were the examination of professional values, professional perspectives on micro and macro issues, and the definition of problems and roles in interprofessional collaboration.

The issue of commitment to the project was brought up numerous times. Maintaining momentum was not easy. The group had periods when it made only limited progress toward its goal. At times, the task appeared endless. Fortunately, individuals' motivation and momentum did not decline simultaneously. The commitment to an agreed-upon outcome that would be the result of an interprofessional process rather than the work of separate authors warranted such effort. However, the writing team had to go through its developmental stages

---

[1] Please refer to Chapter 2 for a discussion of the importance of individual differences and personality types in the interprofessional team.

like any other group. The uniqueness of this team produced a unique process and product at each stage of its work.

The goal of joint authorship of a distinctively interprofessional product provided the rationale for the entire process. Attempting to bring together different minds to produce one common piece of work, as opposed to producing one work containing different pieces, was a difficult challenge. Some have said that only a group of fools would try to accomplish such a task—so we tried!

Index

Abramson, J., 30
Accepted behaviors, 26
Accommodation stage, in group development, 38
Administrative support, 101
Adolescents, 6
AIDS (HIV infection), 11
Allen, A. S., 19, 21, 99, 107
American Association of Colleges for Teacher Education, 104
American Association of Colleges of Nursing, 104
American Bar Association, 104
American Counseling Association, 104
American Medical Association, 104, 144
American Physical Therapy Association, 145
American Psychological Association, 104
Anthony, E. J., 36, 54
Anticipatory guidance, 82, 84
Anticipatory management, 88
Association of American Law Schools, 104
Association of Schools of Allied Health Professions, 104
Association of Theological Schools, 104
Assumptions, professional, 12, 13
Attention deficit disorder, 85, 86
Autonomy, professional, 24, 28, 52

Baldwin, D. C., Jr., 9
Bales, R. F., 49
Balint, M., 88, 92

Barker, L., 35, 55
Barrett, J. A., 92
Barrett, J. E., 92
Barriers, 46
Basuray, J., 108
Battison, S., 109
Baylor University, 107
Becker, H., 25, 26, 30
Becker, M. H., 75, 92, 93
Beckhard, R., 41, 51, 56
Berger, K. S., 75, 92
Billups, J. O., 37, 54, 55, 108
Biosphere, 17
Blank, M. J., 9, 105, 106, 109
Boundaries, professional, 45
Brieland, D., 52, 55
Briggs, T., 52, 55
Brill, N., 38, 49, 51, 52, 53, 55
Brody, D. S., 80, 92
Brody, S., 28, 30
Bronfenbrenner, U., 87, 92
Brown, G., 108
Bruner, C., 105, 108
Brunner, M. L., 140
Brutvan, E. L., 24, 30
Burgess-Ellison, J. A., 55, 98, 99, 109, 168
Burnam, A., 94
Burrow, T., 36

California General Assembly, 107
Caplan, G., 76, 77, 92

TO THE OWNER OF THIS BOOK:

We hope that you have found *Interprofessional Care and Collaborative Practice* useful. So that this book can be improved in a future edition, would you take the time to complete this sheet and return it? Thank you.

School and address: _____

Department: _____

Instructor's name: _____

1. What I like most about this book is: _____

_____

2. What I like least about this book is: _____

_____

3. My general reaction to this book is: _____

_____

4. The name of the course in which I used this book is: _____

_____

5. Were all of the chapters of the book assigned for you to read? _____

   If not, which ones weren't? _____

_____

6. In the space below, or on a separate sheet of paper, please write specific suggestions for improving this book and anything else you'd care to share about your experience in using the book.

_____

_____

_____

_____

_____

_____

Optional:

Your name: _____ Date: _____

May Brooks/Cole quote you either in promotion for *Interprofessional Care and Collaborative Practice* or in future publishing ventures?

Yes: _____ No: _____

Sincerely,

R. Michael Casto and the Commission on Interprofessional Practice

---

Brooks/Cole is dedicated to publishing quality publications for education in the human services fields. If you are interested in learning more about our publications, please fill in your name and address and request our latest catalogue, using this prepaid mailer.

Name: _____

Street Address: _____

City, State, and Zip: _____

FOLD HERE

BUSINESS REPLY MAIL

FIRST CLASS   PERMIT NO. 358   PACIFIC GROVE, CA

POSTAGE WILL BE PAID BY ADDRESSEE

ATT: _____ *Human Services Catalogue*

Brooks/Cole Publishing Company
511 Forest Lodge Road
Pacific Grove, California 93950-9968

FOLD HERE